Shannon Trust Reading Programme

Turning Pages

Getting started

Content

In the first four manuals your Learner was introduced to a phonic approach to reading. They learned to blend letter sounds together to make words and learned some words by sight.

Your Learner will reinforce previous learning and also learn about less common letter combinations and more word endings such as **sion**, **cian** and **ture**.

The main focus of this manual moves from reading single words and sentences to reading longer pieces of text. This will help your Learner to develop more reading stamina. At this stage you can also encourage your Learner to develop other reading strategies that will help them cope with reading in everyday life such as:

- Skimming – briefly looking over text to identify its purpose using the headings and the layout
- Scanning – pinpointing specific bits of information rather than reading every word
- Reading in detail – this is very important for instructions, formal letters, legal documents and financial agreements
- Understanding more complex text and vocabulary
- Recognising different text formats and features, such as headings, bullet points and numbered instructions, and different font styles

You will need to support your Learner to read these longer pieces of text by sharing the reading or reading alongside quietly and explaining unknown words. There is plenty of opportunity in the last part of the manual for discussion, and Learners should be encouraged to ask questions and give their own opinions about the text. You will find more information on shared reading in the introduction to the first manual.

Getting started

Sounds covered in the first four manuals

Sound	Example	Example	Example	Example	Example
a	c**a**t				
b	**b**un	ra**bb**it			
c	**c**ow	lu**ck**	**k**ite		
d	**d**og	a**dd**			
e	l**e**g	h**ea**d			
f	**f**at	sti**ff**			
g	ba**g**	e**gg**	**g**em	**g**yrate	**g**in**g**er
h	**h**and				
i	**i**n				
j	**j**ug	**gi**ant	he**dge**		
l	**l**ip	fu**ll**			
m	**m**en	co**mm**a			
n	**n**ot	su**nn**y			
o	p**o**t				
p	ho**p**	ha**pp**y			
qu	**qu**ick				
r	**r**ib	ho**rr**id			
s	**s**un	me**ss**	**c**ity	ra**c**e	**c**ycle
t	**t**op	po**tt**ed			
u	r**u**n				
v	**v**an				

Getting started

Sounds covered in the first four manuals

Sound	Example	Example	Example	Example	Example
w	**w**in	**w**hen			
x	ta**x**				
y	**y**es				
z	**z**ip	ja**zz**			
th	**th**en	mo**th**			
ch	**ch**op	ma**tch**			
sh	ru**sh**				
ng	ra**ng**				
nk	ra**nk**				
(Long) ā	r**ai**n	d**ay**	t**a**m**e**		
(Long) ē	tr**ee**	t**ea**	ver**y**	**e**v**e**	
(Long) ō	b**oa**t	gr**ow**	n**o**t**e**		
(Long) ī	m**y**	f**igh**t	l**i**k**e**		
(Long) ū	sh**oo**t	b**oo**k	c**ue**	f**ew**	t**u**b**e**
ar	c**ar**d				
er	lett**er**	b**ur**n	b**ir**d		
ow	h**ou**se	c**ow**			
oi	s**oi**l	b**oy**			
or	f**or**	m**or**e	y**aw**n	fr**au**d	
ul	hand**le**	med**al**	skilf**ul**		
air	h**air**	b**are**	w**ear**		

Sound	Example	Example	Example	Example	Example
f	**ph**one				
sh	sta**ti**on	se**ss**ion	musi**ci**an		
zh	televi**si**on				
(Long) ā	**ei**ght	th**ey**	gr**ea**t	**a**ble	
(Long) ē	reli**e**f	k**ey**	m**e**	rec**ei**ve	ser**i**ous
(Long) ō	t**oe**	th**ough**	**o**pen	s**ew**	
(Long) ī	t**ie**	v**i**rus	h**ei**ght		
(Long) ū	s**ou**p	d**o**	s**u**per	s**ui**t	
er	col**our**	doct**or**	**ear**th	coll**ar**	
or	b**oar**d	d**oor**	th**ought**	w**ar**m	c**our**t
ul	petr**ol**	funn**el**	ev**il**		
chur	pic**ture**				

Get started

Sight Words

Remember that some Sight Words do not work well with phonics and are better learned as whole words such as **the**, **some**, **one**, **said**, **all**.

The table below shows the words your Learner has covered so far and the new ones they will learn in this manual.

Sight Words already covered						Sight Words in this manual	
about	done	I	once	the	were	January	father
after	does	I'm	only	their	what	February	son
all	don't	knew	other	there	when	March	daughter
any	down	know	out	they	where	April	auntie
are	for	love	over	Thursday	who	May	nephew
be	Friday	me	people	time	woman	June	niece
because	friend	Monday	put	to	women	July	laugh
before	give	money	said	Tuesday	work	August	enough
buy	go	most	Saturday	two	would	September	won't
call	gone	my	she	use	you	October	wash
come	have	no	so	want	your	November	water
could	he	of	some	was		December	pretty
day	her	old	Sunday	we			
do	here	one	sure	Wednesday			

Get started

Reading longer words: syllables

Learners have learned to break longer words into smaller 'chunks' called syllables and put them back together again to build the whole word.

These 'chunks' are the beats that can be tapped out when a word is read aloud.

Words can be **one syllable** long (one beat) such as: **bed, reach, know, dressed**, or have **two, three, four** or **more** syllables, such as: **to/day, fan/tas/tic, diff/i/cul/ty, or/gan/i/sa/tion.** It doesn't matter too much where a Learner puts the break as long as they get the number of syllables right and each syllable has a vowel.

Mentors can help their Learners by:

- Reading longer words aloud slowly, tapping out each syllable as they say it: **fan/tas/tic** (3 beats)
- Telling their Learner that every syllable has a vowel sound in it. This may be a single vowel: **a**, **e**, **i**, **o**, **u** (**y** can also be a vowel) or a vowel sound made from letter combinations such as: **ai**, **ay**, **ee**, **ea**, **or**, **ar**, **aw**, **igh**, **air**
- Getting them to try the **V**owel, **S**ound, **B**reak (VSB) method with longer words. This method asks the Learner to find the **V**owel sound (there may be more than one); then the letter **S**ound that follows it; and to then mark in the syllable **B**reak (forward slash /) after this sound. This works with words such as: **pan/ic**, **con/tain**, **wis/dom**, **ad/ven/ture**
- Telling them to keep double letters together as one sound such as: **rabb/it**, **miss/ing**
- Uncovering a longer word a bit at a time from left to right, reading each 'chunk' as it appears

Finding more information

You can find more help and information on Turning Pages on the Shannon Trust website including:

- An audio file where you can listen to and practise the sounds chart.
- An audio file where your Learner can listen to and practise the first sounds covered in Turning Pages.
- An audio file with some Top Tips for Mentors.
- A 'letter cards' template.
- Completion certificates.

Get started

Start to read by learning the letter sounds

1. Use the statements on the opposite page to explain to your Learner what they will be learning in this manual.

2. Remind them that you will be covering all the steps in the activities to make sure there are no gaps in their knowledge, and they will have plenty of time to repeat and practise activities when they need to.

3. Tell your Learner that this is the last Turning Pages manual. They will get a chance to practise their reading skills with words, sentences and longer pieces of text.

4. Towards the end of the manual they will be asked to read and understand different types of text that they may need to read in everyday life, such as menus, instructions, letters and general information.

5. Tell your Learner that they will come across text in this manual that uses other font styles.

6. Remind them that it is important that they do not try to rush though the activities. This manual needs lots of focus and concentration.

Tip: A font is a specific typeface of a certain size and style. Such as: **Arial 12 pt bold** or *Times New Roman 14 pt italic*.

Notes:

Get started

In this manual you will:

Keep practising letter sounds and blending to make words.

Understand how different letters can be put together to make new sounds.

Understand that some sounds can be shown in many ways.

Read sentences to decide how some sounds should be pronounced.

Read some words by sight.

Read some longer words, sentences and paragraphs.

Learn some reading strategies that will help you cope with longer pieces of text.

You will be asked to **listen**, **look** and **read** aloud.
You can also have a go at writing words.
There will be lots of chances for you to see how you are getting on and the progress you are making.

Listen and point

Introduce Learners to silent letters

1. Tell your Learner that English is a mixture of many languages such as German, Latin and Greek. This helps to explain:

- The many different spellings of sounds in reading.
- Why there are **silent letters** in some words – at one time they may have been pronounced but over the years have become silent.

2. Point to the letters at the top of each box and tell your Learner that these letters can be silent in some words.

3. Read the words in the 8 boxes to your Learner, pointing out the **blue** letters that they can see but **cannot hear** in the words.

- Point to each word as you read it and ask your Learner to repeat the word.
- Tell them to take particular notice of what they can hear when each word is read. (Sometimes it is the second sound they hear because of a silent letter such as **k** in **k**nife).
- Go through the lists at random saying the words and asking your Learner to find and point to the word in each case.

Tip: Point out that a silent **g** or **k** is always before an **n** as in **gnat** and **knew**. Silent **w** is before **r** as in **wr**ite. The **al** letter combination can be pronounced in different ways as in w**al**k or c**al**m.

Notes:

Listen and point

Learn about silent letters

All the **blue** letters are silent

k

knife
knee
knock
knew

g

gnaw
gnash
si**g**n
gnat

b

thum**b**
dou**b**t
plum**b**er
bom**b**

w

write
wrap
wrestle
s**w**ord

h

hour
g**h**ost
Jo**h**n
sc**h**ool

gh

ni**gh**t
thou**gh**t
dou**gh**
tau**gh**t

l

ta**l**k
yo**l**k
sa**l**mon
cou**l**d
ca**l**m

t

lis**t**en
cas**t**le
whis**t**le
sof**t**en

Listen and point

Learners listen and find the words with a **silent letter**

Words to read

nes/tle	Christ/mas
hour	school
sal/mon	yolk
re/sign	caught
climb	wrist
list/en	knock
knife	numb
hon/est	
bough (like **cow**)	

Tip:

1. Tell your Learner that they will need to use their sounding out skills to find the word on the Learner page that matches what they hear.

2. Read the first word: **nestle**. Sound it out in syllables ***nes/tle*** (the **t** is silent). Say it again as a whole word.
Ask your Learner:

- What is the first syllable you can hear? ***nes***
- What is the next syllable you hear? ***tle*** (***ul***)

3. Ask your Learner to say the word again blending the two syllables: **nestle.**

- Tell them to find the word **nestle** in the grid and tick it.

4. Repeat this process with all the other words.

- Note that only 6 of the words are made up of two syllables. Say the others as whole words.
- Remember **not to sound out** the silent letters (**b**, **g**, **h**, **k**, **l**, **t**, **w**) or combination of silent letters (**gh**).

5. Ask your Learner to look at the words and circle the **silent letters.**

Notes:

Listen and point

Find the words that you hear

Christmas	listen	caught	school
yolk	knock	resign	wrist
climb	knife	numb	nestle
salmon	bough	honest	hour

Read and check

Learners practise reading words and sentences with silent letters

1. Tell your Learner that knowing the meaning of words with silent letters is helpful in deciding how to read them. This is why a sentence is given alongside each word.

2. Ask your Learner to read the first word in the grid: **knew.** Use the sentence with the word in if needed.

3. Ask them to do this with all the other words.

- Tell them that if they are not sure how to read the single words to read the sentence first and then go back to the word.
- Tick all the words they get right. Leave the others blank.

4. When your Learner has finished, go over any words that have not been ticked.

- Ask your Learner to read them again and tick the ones they get right.

5. Make a note of any words that are still a problem in the Notes box.

- Go over these words again once or twice.
- If any words remain a problem, or take two or three tries to get right, add them to the Parking page (page 59).

Tip: Support an ESOL Learner with the pronunciation of d**ou**gh (**ou** sound as in bl**ow**). Ask your Learner to circle all the silent letters in the sentences.

Notes:

Read and check

Check that you can read these words and sentences with silent letters

	✓
knew	
thum**b**	
gnashed	
C**h**ris**t**mas	
wa**l**k	
knock	
honest	
sc**h**ool	
lis**t**en	
dou**gh**	
resi**g**n	
knife	

I knew the man who ran the shop.
He cut his thumb on the broken glass.
The dog gnashed his teeth at the other dog.
Christmas is on 25th December.
I've missed the bus so I will walk into town.
'Knock on Sam's door to see if he's up', said Jill.
Aziz is an honest, hard-working man.
She starts school in September.
If you listen hard you can hear the river.
Is the dough ready for the bread rolls?
The chairman had to resign after all the fuss.
You will need a sharp knife to carve the meat.

Gap fill

Learners read sentences and fill in the missing words

Your Learner may need to read each sentence more than once to get the meaning.

1. Explain to your Learner that they will read some sentences with some words missing. They will choose the right words to complete the sentence.

2. Read out Sentence 1 with the gaps and the words written in brackets:
'__________ train will be here in an __________,' said Sally. (**hour, Our**)

- Show how to complete the sentence by trying each word from the brackets.
- Write the correct words in the spaces.
- Read the sentence again to help your Learner make sense of it:
'Our train will be here in an hour', said Sally.

3. Support your Learner to do the same with the other sentences. Read it with them if needed.

- Each time ask your Learner to try both words to see which one makes sense.

Tip: Support an ESOL Learner with the pronunciation of b**ou**gh (**ou** sound as in c**ow**) and br**ou**ght (**ou** sound as in l**aw**). Point out the silent **h** and **t** in w**h**is**t**le.

Notes:

Gap fill

Complete these sentences so that they make sense

1.	'______________ train will be here in an ______________,' said Sally.	(hour, Our)
2.	My kids ______________ to ______________ every Monday and Friday.	(walk, school)
3.	The party host said there was a ______________ in the ______________.	(castle, ghost)
4.	John said he would ______________ to her every week while he was in ______________.	(Wrexham, write)
5.	A huge ______________ fell off the tree and ______________ the fence down.	(bough, brought)
6.	It was a thumbs-up for the ______________ team as the ______________ blew for the end of the match.	(whistle, Norfolk)
7.	A loud ______________ at the door made the dog growl and ______________ his teeth.	(gnash, knock)
8.	The fisherman showed the young lad how to ______________ the ______________.	(fasten, dinghy)

Text and check

Learners read sentences that include words with silent letters

1. Ask your Learner to read the sentences in the text.
- Tick all the ones they get right and leave the others blank.

2. Go over any sentences that have not been ticked.
- Underline any errors in each sentence.
- Read them to your Learner and sound them out. (Do not sound out Sight Words or silent letters.)
- Ask your Learner to read the sentences again and tick the ones they get right.
- Point out the apostrophe in Sentences 2 and 6 (wren's, John's) which means belonging to.

3. Make a note of any words that are still a problem in the Notes box. Go over these words once or twice.
- If any words remain a problem, or take two or three tries to get right, add them to the Parking page (page 59).

4. Ask questions about the sentences to check understanding, such as: Who is likely to be running a campaign? What was the cook doing when he cut his thumb?

Tip:

Notes:

Text and check

Read some sentences that include words with silent letters

	✓
He knew that walking down the steep mountain would hurt his knees.	
A little wren's nest nestled among the leaves and moss in the grassy bank.	
The campaign was thought to have been an honest one, run by a political party that could listen and talk to a wide range of people.	
The cook cut his thumb when he was sharpening his knife.	
The schoolchildren knew that the gates to the castle would be fastened after 5 o'clock.	
John's legs had gone numb after he knelt for too long fixing the brakes on the car.	
She always had to wrestle with what to say before she could write anything down.	
There was a ghastly whistle as the bomb dropped.	

Spot the word

Learners look for the months of the year

Your Learner may already know some of these words.

1. Read the words: **January**, **February**, **March**, **April**, **May**, **June**, **July**, **August**, **September**, **October**, **November**, **December**.

- Point out that the months of the year all start with a capital letter.
- Ask your Learner to read the words.
- Point to words in random order and ask your Learner to read them to you.

2. Explain to your Learner that they will be looking for the months of the year in the text on the Learner page.

- Read the first sentence and point out the word: **January**. Underline the word.
- Tell your Learner to read the next sentence and find the months: **January**, **February** and **March**.
- Ask them to underline each one.

3. Ask your Learner to read the rest of the text and underline the months of the year as they read.

4. Finish the task by counting how many times each month appears in the text. Write the number next to each month: **January** (3), **February** (1), **March** (4), **April** (1), **May** (1), **June** (2), **July** (1), **August** (1), **September** (1), **October** (3), **November** (2), **December** (1).

Tip: Point out the colon in the first sentence. Explain these are used to introduce a list of items, a definition, statement or explanation.

Notes:

Spot the word

Find the months of the year

January	
February	
March	
April	
May	
June	
July	
August	
September	
October	
November	
December	

January 1st is New Year's Day in this country: a time to make plans for the year ahead.

January, February and March have long dark days when it seems that winter will never end. Then spring comes in April and May and we forget about the cold January days and the wind in March.

June, July and August are best with hot sunshine and long sunny days but summer is soon over.

Autumn comes in September, October and November when the leaves fall off the trees. The days get shorter in October when the clocks go back. I don't like the long winter nights from October to March.

I love December because it's Christmas. Sometimes it snows. In the north the snow can last from November to March.

My birthday is in June. It's in the middle of the year so that's something for me to look forward to.

Read and check

Learners practise reading the months of the year

1. Remind your Learner that the words in the grid need to be remembered as whole words not sounded out.

2. Ask your Learner to read each word in the grid.

- Tell them to tick all the words they get right and leave the others blank.

3. When your Learner has finished, go over any words that have not been ticked:

- Read them to your Learner (do not sound them out).
- Ask your Learner to read them again and tick the ones they get right.

4. If any words remain a problem, or take two or three tries to get right, write them in the Notes box and practise them with 'Look and Say, Copy and Say' (as you do on the Parking page) until your Learner is confident.

Tip:

Notes:

Read and check

Check that you can read the months of the year

	✓
January	
February	
March	
April	
May	
June	
July	
August	
September	
October	
November	
December	
April	
July	

	✓
May	
January	
July	
August	
October	
April	
February	
September	
November	
February	
March	
June	
December	
October	

Text and check

Learners read sentences with the months of the year

1. Ask your Learner to read the months of the year.
- Practise the words with your Learner if you need to.

2. Ask your Learner to read the sentences in the grid.
- Tick all the ones they get right and leave the others blank.

3. Go over any sentences that have not been ticked.
- Underline any errors in each sentence.
- Read them to your Learner.
- Ask your Learner to read the sentences again and to tick the ones they get right.

4. Make a note of any words that are a problem in the Notes box. Go over these once or twice.
- If any words remain a problem, or take two or three tries to get right, add them to the Parking page (page 59).

5. Ask some questions about the sentences to check understanding, such as: Why didn't they go on honeymoon straight away? How many times do they have to go to the hospital?

Tip:

Notes:

Text and check

Read some sentences with months of the year

January
February
March
April
May
June
July
August
September
October
November
December

	✓
We were engaged in February and got married in November. We couldn't afford a honeymoon until the next July.	
The football season starts in August and finishes at the end of May but there are matches all year round.	
In January and February some people get depressed because there is no sunshine.	
The apple blossom is out in April and May and the roses come out in June.	
The school summer holiday starts in July and goes on to the beginning of September.	
I have to go back to the hospital in April, June and December.	
The clocks go back in October and go forward in March.	
There are two bank holidays in May and one at the end of August.	
Sam was born in December, Pat was born in March and Asha was born in January.	
I start my Christmas shopping in September and spread the cost through October and November.	

Listen and point

Introduce Learners to the **f** sound: **ph**, **f**

1. Remind your Learner that some letters and letter combinations look different but sound the same such as ***e*** in b**e**d and ***ea*** in br**ea**d.

2. Tell your Learner that they are going to learn about **ph** which sounds the same as ***f***.
- Point to **ph** above the list on the Learner page and read the words.
- Ask your Learner to read the words.
- Go through the list at random, saying the words. Ask your Learner to find and point to the correct word in each case.

3. Point to the list of words that uses the more familiar ***f*** sound.
- Ask your Learner to read the words.
- Tell your Learner that **f** is the most commonly used letter for the ***f*** sound.

4. Read words from both lists at random and ask your Learner to find them.

5. Ask your Learner to read the sentences in the middle of the page.

6. Read the other way to represent the ***f*** sound at the bottom of the page: **gh**. Point out that it appears at the end of this small group of words.

Tip: It can help Learners to remember things if the information becomes more 'memorable'. Tell your Learner that the ***ph*** sound is a part of our language 'borrowed' from the Greeks.

Notes:

Listen and point

Listen for the **f** sound: **ph**, **f**

The letters in bold make a **f** sound

ph	**f**
phone	**f**rantic
phase	**f**arm
ne**ph**ew	lea**f**
or**ph**an	tra**ff**ic
physics	**f**rom
Philip	**f**ilter
al**ph**abet	stu**ff**
ele**ph**ant	**f**ell
tro**ph**y	li**f**ted
photo	terri**f**ic

He could not hear the **ph**one because he was dea**f**.

Fran's ne**ph**ew took her to see **Ph**antom of the Opera last **F**ebruary.

The **f** sound can also be spelt with **gh** as in: rou**gh**, tou**gh**, enou**gh**, cou**gh**, trou**gh.**

Read and check

Learners practise reading words with the **f** sound: **ph**

1. Ask your Learner to read each word in the grid.
- Tick the ones they get right. Leave the others blank.

2. When your Learner has finished, go over any words that have not been ticked.
- Read each of these words and sound them out and read again.
- Ask your Learner to read them again and tick the ones they get right.

3. Make a note of any words that are still a problem in the Notes box.
- Go over these words again once or twice.
- If any words remain a problem, or take two or three tries to get right, write them in the Notes box and practise them with 'Look and Say, Copy and Say' as you do on the Parking page until your Learner is confident.

4. Discuss the meanings of the words with your Learner.

Tip: Some accents may also say the ***f*** sound for ***th*** such as: **th**ink/**f**ink which is fine for them but is not standard phonics.

Notes:

Read and check

Check that you can read these words with the **f** sound: **ph**

	✓
phone	
pharmacy	
alphabet	
phonic	
Philip	
graph	
nephew	
phase	
physics	
geography	

	✓
phantom	
physical	
orphan	
elephant	
pheasant	
photograph	
paragraph	
triumph	
graphic	
dolphin	

Text and check

Learners read sentences that include words with the **f** sound: **ph**

1. Ask your Learner to read the sentences in the grid.

- Tick all the ones they get right and leave the others blank.

2. Go over sentences that have not been ticked.

- Underline any errors in each sentence.
- Read them to your Learner.
- Ask your Learner to read the sentences again and tick the ones they get right.

3. Make a note of any words that are still a problem in the Notes box. Go over these words once or twice.

- If any words remain a problem, or take two or three tries to get right, add them to the Parking page (page 59).

4. Ask some questions about the sentences to check understanding, such as: Where was the baby elephant taken to? What did the farm lads win? What is a pamphlet? (A leaflet or small brochure.)

Tip:

Notes:

Text and check

Read sentences that have words with the **f** sound: **ph**

	✓
Fred had to use the phone in the hospital as his mobile was not working.	
Philip and Frank were the only nephews that their Uncle Ralph saw more than once a year.	
The orphaned baby elephant was taken to an animal rescue centre in Kenya.	
A school of dolphins raced alongside the schooner in the South Pacific Sea.	
Could you hand out these pamphlets to people as they come out of the pharmacy?	
Joseph knew that he needed some physical exercise to help him get fit.	
Freddie's photographs and autographs of sixties bands reminded him of that exciting phase in his life.	
The farm lads held the trophy aloft as they celebrated their triumph in the ploughing competition.	
The atmosphere became hostile when Stephen began to lose his temper.	

Listen and point

Introduce Learners to the **sh** and **zh** sounds: **ti**, **si**, **ssi**, **ci**

1. Tell your Learner they will now learn more about the ***sh*** sound.

- Remind them that until now the sound ***sh*** has been represented by the letters **sh** as in **sh**ip and cra**sh**. This is the most common way of spelling it.

2. Explain to your Learner that the sound ***sh*** can be represented by different letter combinations in the last syllable of words. All the words in this section have more than one syllable.

3. Point to the letter combinations **ti**, **si**, **ssi**, **ci** and say the sound: ***sh***

- Explain that they are spelt differently but they all make the same ***sh*** sound
- Read through the three lists of words emphasising the ***sh*** sound.

4. Now go through the **ti** list with your Learner:

- Point to each word as you read it and ask your Learner to repeat the word.
- Go through the same list at random saying the words. Ask your Learner to find and point to the word in each case.

5. Repeat these activities with the other lists: **si**, **ssi** and **ci**.

Tip: Point out that in some words where the last syllable is **sion,** the **si** is pronounced: ***zh,*** as in **television**, **version**, **explosion**, **Asian**, **fusion**.

Notes:

Listen and point

Find the words with the **sh** and **zh** sounds

All the letters in bold say **sh** or **zh**

ti	**si ssi**	**ci**
sta**ti**on	ten**si**on	so**ci**al
pa**ti**ent	pen**si**on	spe**ci**al
ac**ti**on	mi**ssi**on	deli**ci**ous
men**ti**on	pa**ssi**on	offi**ci**al
atten**ti**on	permi**ssi**on	musi**ci**an
na**ti**on	televi**si**on	cru**ci**al
direc**ti**on	ver**si**on	pre**ci**ous
sec**ti**on	explo**si**on	finan**ci**al

Listen and point

Learners listen and find the words with the **sh** and **zh** sounds: **ti**, **si**, **ssi**, **ci**

Words to read

per/mi/ssion
e/lec/tri/cian
mus/i/cian
ex/ten/sion
sat/is/fac/tion
ex/plo/sion
te/le/vi/sion
su/ffi/cient
ac/tion
spa/cious
de/pre/ssion
sus/pi/cious

Tip: Remind your Learner that in some words, single vowels make a **long vowel sound** in multi-syllable words such as: d**ē**pression, sp**ā**cious, expl**ō**sion.

1. Tell your Learner that they will need to use their sounding out skills to find the word on the Learner page that matches what they hear.

- Tell them they need to listen first and find the word when you ask them to.

2. Read the first word in the Words to read box.

- Say the word: **permission**.
- Sound it out in syllables: ***per/mi/ssion***. (**ssion** said as ***shun***)
- Say it again as a whole word.

3. Show your Learner the grid and ask them to find the word. Say the whole word again if needed.

- Ask them to read the syllables that make up the word, read the whole word again and tick the column if they get it right.

4. Repeat this process with all the other words. Any unticked words can be added to the Notes box and practised again.

Notes:

Listen and point

Find the words that you hear with the **sh** and **zh** sounds: **ti, si, ssi, ci**

						✓
permission	per	mi	ssion		permission	
electrician	e	lec	tri	cian	electrician	
action	ac	tion			action	
television	te	le	vi	sion	television	
satisfaction	sat	is	fac	tion	satisfaction	
explosion	ex	plo	sion		explosion	
spacious	spa	cious			spacious	
suspicious	sus	pi	cious		suspicious	
musician	mus	i	cian		musician	
depression	de	pre	ssion		depression	
sufficient	su	ffi	cient		sufficient	
extension	ex	ten	sion		extension	

Read and check

Learners practise reading words with the **sh** and **zh** sounds: **ti**, **si**, **ssi**, **ci**

1. Ask your Learner to read each word in the grid.
- Tick all the words they get right. Leave the others blank.

2. When your Learner has finished, go over any words that have not been ticked.
- Read each of these words and sound them out as syllables and read again.
- Ask your Learner to read them again and tick the ones they get right.

3. Make a note of any words that are still a problem in the Notes box.
- Go over these words again once or twice.
- If any words remain a problem, or take two or three tries to get right, write them in the Notes box and practise them with 'Look and Say, Copy and Say' as you do on the Parking page until your Learner is confident.

Tip: As extra activities you can ask your Learner to count the number of syllables in each word and also discuss the meanings of the words.

Notes:

Read and check

Check that you can read these words with the **sh** and **zh** sounds: **ti**, **si**, **ssi**, **ci**

	✓
station	
television	
profession	
pension	
impression	
action	
special	
extension	
information	
precious	
depression	
ambition	

	✓
patient	
permission	
option	
decision	
station	
division	
official	
competition	
confession	
direction	
collision	
sensation	

Text and check

Learners read a paragraph that includes words with the **sh** and **zh** sounds: **ti**, **si**, **ssi**, **ci**

The sentences on the Learner page are all part of one paragraph.

1. Ask your Learner to read the sentences in the text.
- Tick all the ones they get right and leave the others blank.

2. Go over sentences that have not been ticked.
- Underline any errors in each sentence.
- Read them to your Learner.
- Ask your Learner to read the sentences again and tick the ones they get right.

3. Make a note of any words that are still a problem in the Notes box. Go over these words once or twice.
- If any words remain a problem, or take two or three tries to get right, add them to the Parking page (page 59).

4. Ask some questions about the paragraph to check understanding, such as: Who owned the mansion? What does it mean by media invasion? (Lots of TV, newspaper and radio reporters rushing to talk to Neesha.)

Tip:

Notes:

Text and check

Read text that has words with the **sh** and **zh** sounds: **ti**, **si**, **ssi**, **ci**

	✓
It was a special day for Neesha. She was going to appear on television.	
She had been asked to explain about the explosion in the mansion house owned by a politician.	
Neesha felt the tension rising. She hoped that she would provide sufficient evidence to help the police in their investigation.	
There had not been any other occasion when Neesha had felt all the attention was just on her.	
She also did not know that there would be a media invasion after her session on TV.	
Neesha took a deep breath as she heard, 'Lights, camera, action ...'	

Spot the word

Learners look for the Sight Words: **father**, **son**, **daughter**, **auntie**, **nephew**, **niece**

1. Read the words: **father, son, daughter, auntie, nephew, niece**
- Ask your Learner to read the words.

2. Show your Learner how to search the small boxes for the word: **father**
- Tick the word every time you find it (there are 4). Write the number on the notepad.

3. Ask your Learner to search the small boxes for the word: **son**
- Point out that this a short word beginning with **s**.
- Tick the word every time they find it (there are 3). Write the number on the notepad.

4. Do the same for the other words: **daughter** (3), **auntie** (2), **nephew** (2), **niece** (3).

5. Point out to your Learner that they can already read the words **mother** and **brother** because they have the same spelling pattern as **other.**
- These words are also hidden on the page. Ask your Learner to find them.

Tip: Auntie can also be spelt **aunty**: **A**untie June, **A**unty June. Auntie and uncle are spelt with a capital letter if the person is named.

Notes:

Spot the word

Read and match Sight Words about family

father son daughter auntie nephew niece

niece

nephew

niece

son

daughter

father

son

nephew

father

daughter

brother

father

daughter

son

niece

mother

auntie

father

auntie

father ____________

son ____________

daughter ____________

auntie ____________

nephew ____________

niece ____________

Read and check

Learners practise reading Sight Words about family

This grid also includes words from previous manuals such as **mother** and **brother**.

1. Ask your Learner to read each word in the grid.

- Tell them to tick all the words they get right and leave the others blank.

2. When your Learner has finished, go over any words that have not been ticked:

- Read them to your Learner (do not sound them out).
- Ask your Learner to read them again and tick the ones they get right.

3. If any words remain a problem, or take two or three tries to get right, write them in the Notes box and practise them with 'Look and Say, Copy and Say' until your Learner is confident.

Tip:

Notes:

Read and check

Check that you can read these Sight Words about family

	✓
father	
son	
mother	
daughter	
auntie	
nephew	
niece	
brother	
son	
auntie	
father	
daughter	
mother	

	✓
nephew	
niece	
mother	
son	
daughter	
father	
auntie	
daughter	
father	
son	
niece	
nephew	
auntie	

Text and check

Learners read sentences with Sight Words about families

1. Ask your Learner to read the Sight Words: **father, son, daughter, auntie, nephew, niece**
- Practise the words with your Learner if you need to.

2. Ask your Learner to read the sentences in the grid.
- Tick all the ones they get right and leave the others blank.

3. Go over any sentences that have not been ticked.
- Underline any errors in each sentence.
- Read them to your Learner.
- Ask your Learner to read the sentences again and to tick the ones they get right.

4. Make a note of any words that are a problem in the Notes box. Go over these once or twice.
- If any words remain a problem, or take two or three tries to get right, add them to the Parking page (page 59).

5. Ask some questions about the sentences to check understanding such as: Who lives with their grandmother in India? How many children did the proud father have altogether?

Tip: Point out the apostrophe which means belonging to, such as: My mother's sister is my auntie.

Notes:

Text and check

Read some sentences with Sight Words about families

father son daughter auntie nephew niece

	✓
My auntie is coming to see us this Tuesday with her son and her daughter.	
My mother's sister is my auntie. My mother's brother is my uncle.	
My father looked after his mother until she died last December.	
'Your daughter looks just like Auntie Grace,' said Auntie May.	
My nephew and my niece live in India with their grandmother.	
I miss my father but I get on well with my stepfather too.	
The wedding was a good chance to meet my auntie and uncle from Canada.	
My sister's son is my only nephew. My brother's daughter is my only niece.	
He was the proud father of three sons and three daughters.	

Listen and point

Introduce Learners to the **chur** and **ch** sounds: **ture, ch**

1. Tell your Learner that there are some words that end with **ture**.

- The **t** in ***t**ure* sounds like ***ch***.
- ***ture*** sounds like ***chur*** as in church.

2. Point to the **ture** spelling on the Learner page and read the words, emphasising the ***chur*** sound at the end of each word.

- Ask your Learner to read the words.

3. Point to the easily recognised **ch** list of words and ask your Learner to read them.

- Go through each list of words at random, saying the words.
- Ask your Learner to find and point to the correct word in each case.

4. Point out that the letter combination: **ture** is at the **end** of words with more than one syllable. The letter combination **ch** can be found anywhere in a word.

Tip: Some accents will say the word ending in **nature** the same as they do in **mature**.

Notes:

Listen and point

Listen for the **chur** and **ch** sounds

The letters in bold say the **ch** sound

ture	**ch**
pic**t**ure	mar**ch**
cap**t**ure	**ch**ain
mix**t**ure	tea**ch**
frac**t**ure	**ch**eek
lec**t**ure	**ch**ildren
adven**t**ure	pun**ch**
prema**t**ure	rea**ch**

Listen and point

Learners listen and find words with the **chur** and **ch** sounds: **ture**, **ch**

Words to read

frac/ture	pic/ture
lunch	chall/enge
crea/ture	chance
reach	mix/ture
chil/dren	fur/ni/ture
teach/ing	cheek
ad/ven/ture	fu/ture
na/ture	ex/change

Tip:

1. Tell your Learner that they will need to use their sounding out skills to find the word on the Learner page that matches what they hear.

2. Read the first word: **fracture**. Sound it out in syllables: ***frac/ture.*** Say it again as a whole word.
   Ask your Learner:

- What is the first syllable you can hear? ***frac***
- What is the last syllable you can hear? ***ture*** (sounds like ***chur***)

3. Ask your Learner to say the word again blending the two syllables: **fracture**.

- Tell them to find the word **fracture** in the grid and tick it.
- Remind your Learner that the ***ture*** (***chur***) sound only appears at the end of words.

4. Repeat the process with all the other words.

- Read one-syllable words such as **lunch** as a whole word. Do not break it down.

5. Ask your Learner to find and underline the ***ture*** endings.

Notes:

Listen and point

Find the words that you hear

fracture	teaching	mixture	reach
cheek	picture	children	future
furniture	chance	adventure	nature
exchange	creature	lunch	challenge

Gap fill

Learners complete words that have the **chur** sound at the end: **ture**

Words to read

mix/ture	fu/ture
pic/ture	den/tures
frac/ture	lec/ture
na/ture	rup/ture
fix/ture	crea/ture
cap/ture	ad/ven/ture

Tip: Sound out **individual** letters that go before the ***ture*** sound if your Learner has difficulty working out the order of the letters. Use letter cards so these letters can be moved around.

1. Ask your Learner to look at the grid with the heading: ***ture.***

- Ask them to read the ***ture*** sound in the heading: ***ture*** (***chur*** as in **chur**ch).

2. Read the first word: **mixture.** Sound it out in syllables*:* ***mix/ture.***

- Show your Learner how to complete the word using the letters given.
- Write in the letters and ask your Learner to read the whole word: **mixture**.

3. Take one word at a time in the list:

- Read it and sound it out in syllables (remember to say ***ture*** as one sound).
- Ask your Learner to use the letters given to complete each word.
- Encourage them to do the writing.
- You may need to repeat the words more than once.
- Point out that all the words with **ture** on the end have more than one syllable.

Notes:

Gap fill

Use the letters to complete words with the **chur** sound at the end: **ture**

ture			
x i m	__ __ __ ture	u f	__ __ ture
p c i	__ __ __ ture	d n e s	__ __ __ ture __
f a r c	__ __ __ __ ture	e c l	__ __ __ ture
a n	__ __ ture	u r p	__ __ __ ture
i f x	__ __ __ ture	c ea r	__ __ ___ ture
a c p	__ __ __ ture	a d e v n	__ __ __ __ __ ture

Read and check

Learners practise reading words with the **chur** sound at the end: **ture**

1. Ask your Learner to read each word in the grid.
- Tick the words they get right. Leave the others blank.

2. When your Learner has finished, go over any words that have not been ticked.
- Read each of these words and sound them out, syllable by syllable.
- Support your Learner with multi-syllable words if they need it. Read each word aloud slowly tapping out each syllable as you say it.
- Mark in the syllable breaks with a slash.
- Ask your Learner to read the word again and tick the ones they get right.

3. If any words remain a problem, or take two or three tries to get right, write them in the Notes box and practise them with 'Look and Say, Copy and Say' until your Learner is confident.

Tip: Ask your Learner if there are any words that they do not understand. Explain the meanings of the words.

Notes:

Read and check

Check that you can read these words with the **chur** sound at the end: **ture**

	✓
ven**ture**	
lec**ture**	
na**ture**	
cul**ture**	
mix**ture**	
tex**ture**	
adven**ture**	
litera**ture**	
frac**ture**	
sta**ture**	
ma**ture**	
signa**ture**	

	✓
crea**ture**	
fea**ture**	
furni**ture**	
prema**ture**	
fu**ture**	
manufac**ture**	
struc**ture**	
punc**ture**	
den**ture**s	
fix**ture**	
pic**ture**	
scrip**ture**	

Text and check

Learners read text that includes words with the **chur** sound: **ture**

1. Ask your Learner to read the text on the Learner page.

- Tick all the sentences they get right and leave the others blank.

2. Go over the sentences that have not been ticked.

- Underline any errors in each sentence.
- Read them to your Learner. Sound out the syllables slowly, tapping each one out as you say it. Mark the syllable breaks. (**Him/a/lay/as**, **ex/hi/bi/tion**)
- Ask your Learner to read the word again.
- Ask your Learner to read the sentences again and tick the ones they get right.

3. Make a note of any words that are still a problem in the Notes box. Go over these words once or twice.

- If any words remain a problem, or take two or three tries to get right, add them to the Parking page (page 59).

4. Ask your Learner to retell the story in their own words to check understanding.

Tip: It can help to cover up the text not being read, so that your Learner can focus on one sentence at a time.

Notes:

Text and check

Read some sentences using words with the **chur** sound: **ture**

	✓
Mansur put his signature at the bottom of the form and knew that he was in for the adventure of his life.	
The future looked bright and hopeful for him at last.	
Mansur had signed up for a trek with a mixture of other young people into the Himalayas.	
At the lecture they had been told that the air was thin and it could drop to below freezing at night.	
Walking about twelve miles a day at this altitude would be a challenge but they would follow this structure for the whole trek.	
They were all to take a camera to capture what they saw in nature. These could be mountain features or creatures.	
An exhibition of their photos would be shown at the Natural History Museum in London.	
Mansur took home all the pictures and literature about the trek. He could not wait for September to come.	

Parking page

Use the page opposite to note down any sounds or words you have come across in the manual that your Learner needs to practise again. Do this activity when you have completed all the other activities.

1. Write the words in the first (Park) column as you come across them in the manual.

2. When you and your Learner get to this page:

- Take **one** word at a time.
- Read it to your Learner and sound it out (Note: Sight Words are **not** sounded out).
- Ask your Learner to read the whole word.
- Ask your Learner to copy the word and say it.
- Tick it if they get it right.
- Repeat the whole process with the same word: Copy and Say, Copy and Say until they are confident with it. Repeat on a new row if you need to.

3. Repeat the 'Look and Say, Copy and Say' process with all the other words in the Park column.

4. If your Learner continues to struggle with a word, make sure they know what the words means and try putting it into sentences for them.

Tip:

Notes:

Parking page

Park. Look and Say	✓

Copy and Say	✓

Copy and Say	✓

Copy and Say	✓

Parking page

Use the page opposite to note down any more words your Learner needs to practise again. Treat in the same way as outlined on the previous Parking page.

Tip:

Notes:

Park. Look and Say	✓

Copy and Say	✓

Copy and Say	✓

Copy and Say	✓

Progress check

Explain to your Learner that this is a good point in the programme to see how things are going.

Ask your Learner to read each word in the Progress check.

- Tick everything they get right.
- Leave blank any words that your Learner cannot read.
- Use the Turning Pages Reading Levels to show your Learner how much they have achieved.
- Keep a note of any words or letter sounds they are not confident with. Your Learner can practise them at the beginning of the next session.

Note: The sentences in the first grid are there to support your Learner by providing a context for the words with silent letters. The sentences do not need to be marked.

Turning Pages Reading Levels

All or most of the words with **silent letters** read correctly. (No more than 5 errors.)	**TP Level 5.1**
All or most of the words with the ***ph*** sound read correctly. (No more than 3 errors.)	**TP Level 5.2**

Tip:

Notes:

Progress check

Read and tick all the words you know:

		✓
knee	I fell and hurt my knee.	
signs	He followed the road signs.	
thumb	The toddler sucked his thumb.	
write	I will write a thank-you letter.	
ghost	She loved ghost stories.	
school	Fred is always late for school.	
thought	We thought the team would win.	
talk	Can you talk to him on the phone?	
listen	'Listen to what I say!'	
Christmas	My nan is coming for Christmas.	
knife	The knife is too blunt to cut anything.	
hour	He'll be here in an hour.	

TP Level 5.1 ☐

	✓
phone	
elephant	
alphabet	
Philip	
photo	
phobia	
orphan	
graphic	
dolphin	
graph	
pharmacy	
physics	

TP Level 5.2 ☐

Progress check

Ask your Learner to read each word in the Progress check.

- Tick everything they get right.
- Leave blank any words that your Learner cannot read.
- Use the Turning Pages Reading Levels to show your Learner how much they have achieved.
- Keep a note of any words or letter sounds they are not confident with. Your Learner can practise them at the beginning of the next session.

Turning Pages Reading Levels

All or most of the words with the ***sh*** sound read correctly. (No more than 5 errors.)	**TP Level 5.3**
All or most of the words with the **ture** ending read correctly. (No more than 3 errors.)	**TP Level 5.4**

Tip:

Notes:

Progress check

Read and tick all the words you know:

	✓		✓
station		facial	
action		explosion	
television		mention	
permission		confession	
special		relation	
social		information	
section		decision	
pension		delicious	
passion		profession	
official		depression	
direction		collision	
ration		option	

TP Level 5.3 ☐

	✓
picture	
creature	
nature	
future	
mixture	
fracture	
adventure	
mature	
puncture	
denture	
furniture	
signature	

TP Level 5.4 ☐

Progress check

Ask your Learner to read all the sentences in the Progress check.

- Tick everything they get right.
- Underline any errors in the sentences.
- Use the Turning Pages Reading Levels to show your Learner how much they have achieved.
- Keep a note of any words or letter sounds they are not confident with. Your Learner can practise them at the beginning of the next session.

Turning Pages Reading Levels

All or most of the sentences read correctly. (No more than 5 errors.)	**TP Level 5.5**

If your Learner makes more than 15 errors overall (in both words and sentences) **you will need to go over the relevant activities again and spend some more time practising with the Turning Pages reading books. When you have done this, try the Progress check again.**

Tip:

Notes:

Progress check

Read these sentences

My mother and father were married in September.	
The summer session of parliament starts in June and finishes in the middle of July.	
My son had to wait from January until August for a decision about his promotion.	
We are looking after my daughter's dog in April and May.	
My nephew and niece are coming to stay in December.	
My auntie is going on an adventure in March to swim with the dolphins in Florida.	
Lots of people get winter depression in February. It's called Seasonal Affective Disorder or SAD for short.	
The sea gets colder from November to March.	
There will be a new sports channel on television in October.	

TP Level 5.5 ☐

Progress check feedback

The Turning Pages Reading Levels show your Learner what they have achieved.

Congratulate them and explain what each level means.

Ask your Learner if there any words that they would like to go over again. Make a note of them below.

Go over them before moving on.

Your Learner has achieved the skills to read all the Turning Pages reading books and other emergent reader materials available from the library.

Tip:

Notes:

Congratulations!

You are reading words and sentences with different endings and silent letters. You are also reading more Sight Words including the months of the year.

You are now reading at **TP Level 5.5**

Next we are going to look at:

- More vowel sounds
- More Sight Words
- Longer pieces of text

Listen and point

Learners listen and find words with the **long ā** sound.

1. Tell your Learner they are going to learn more about the **long ā** sound. Remind them of the letter combinations they have already learned: **ay** (d**ay**), **ai** (p**ai**n), **a _ e** (g**a**t**e**).

- Ask your Learner to read the three lists at the top of the Learner page: **ay**, **ai** and **a _ e**.

2. Point out to your Learner that there are other letter combinations that also make a **long ā** sound: **ei, ey, ea** and **a** (all pronounced with **long ā**). Explain that these are less common.

- Point to the letter combination **ei** and say the sound: **ā**
- Read the **ei** list of words emphasising the long **ā** sound.
- Point to each word as you read it and ask your Learner to repeat the word.
- Go through the same list at random, say the words and ask your Learner to find and point to the correct word in each case.

3. Now go through the other lists in the same way.

4. Read words from any of the lists at random and ask your Learner to find and point to the correct word in each case.

Tip: Point out the silent letters in the **ei** column – **eigh** is a spelling pattern that is easy to spot. Discuss the meaning: **reins** (used to guide a horse) and **reigns** (the Queen reigns over us).

Notes:

Listen and point

Learn more about the **long ā** sound

ay	ai	a _ e
d**ay**	p**ai**n	l**a**t**e**
s**ay**	m**ai**nt**ai**n	cr**a**n**e**
del**ay**	tr**ai**n	bl**a**m**e**
tr**ay**	**ai**m	beh**a**v**e**
m**ay**be	str**ai**ght	esc**a**p**e**

All the letters in bold say **long a**

ei	ey	ea	a
eight	th**ey**	gr**ea**t	**a**pron
w**eigh**t	pr**ey**	br**ea**k	**a**ble
w**eigh**	conv**ey**	st**ea**k	**a**corn
r**ei**ns	surv**ey**		n**a**tion
r**ei**gn			

Read and check

Learners practise reading words with the **long ā** sound

1. Point out to your Learner that all the words in the grid have a **long ā** sound.
- These are represented by the different letter combinations shown at the top of the page.

2. Ask your Learner to read each word in the grid.
- Tick all the words they get right. Leave the others blank.

3. When your Learner has finished, go over any words that have not been ticked.
- Read each of these words and sound them out and read again.
- Ask your Learner to read them again and tick the ones they get right.

4. Make a note of any words that are still a problem in the Notes box.
- Go over these words again once or twice.
- If any words remain a problem, or take two or three tries to get right, add them to the blank column on page 77.

Tip:

Notes:

Read and check

Check that you can read these words with the **long ā** sound

ay ai a _ e ei ey ea a

	✓
Sund**ay**	
tr**ai**l	
r**a**dio	
eight	
ag**e**	
cl**ai**m	
g**a**m**e**	
conv**ey**	
apron	
tod**ay**	
b**a**sic	
gr**ea**t	
str**ai**ght	

	✓
trade	
stay	
baby	
maintain	
weight	
they	
eighteen	
vein	
insane	
paper	
Spain	
break	
maybe	

	✓
survey	
indicate	
reign	
display	
April	
freight	
danger	
explain	
save	
chain	
taken	
steak	
praise	

Spot the sound

Learners look for the letter combinations that make the **long ā** sound

The first part of the text has been marked as an example.

1. Remind your Learner of all the different letter combinations that can make the **long *ā*** sound.

- Tell them that they will be looking for these letter combinations in the text on the Learner page.

2. Read through the first 4 lines of the text and point out the letter combinations that make **long *ā***. These have been marked in bold.

3. Ask your Learner to read the rest of the text with you. This can be done by quietly reading as your Learner reads or by sharing the reading – read a sentence each.

- Ask them to look over the text again and underline any of the **long *ā*** sounds they can find.
- Show your Learner how to track along each line using their finger. This will help them to find the **long *ā***.

Tip: The sound ***ur*** made with the letters **ear** is new to your Learner. Point this out in the first sentence: **earth.** Ask your Learner if this text is true (fact) or has been made up (fiction). (It is fact.)

Notes:

Spot the sound

Find the **long a** sound

ay	**ai**	**a _ e**	**ei**	**ey**	**ea**	**a**

Sp**ace** St**a**tion

The International Sp**ace** St**a**tion (ISS) orbits the earth about 15 times a d**ay**.

It m**ai**nt**ai**ns an altitude of about 200 to 250 miles from our planet.

The International Sp**ace** St**a**tion has a crew of six to **ei**ght people. Th**ey** st**ay** on board for several months in a st**ate** of w**ei**ghtlessness.

The crew are trained to carry out everyday tasks while they are weightless.

They complete experiments and carry out surveys in space that cannot be done on earth. They also have to maintain the space station. They may have to do a space walk to fix things outside the spacecraft if something breaks.

The greatest danger is being hit by other objects in space in which case they have to evacuate straight away in an escape shuttle.

Read and check

Learners practise reading words with the **long ā** sound

1. Point out to your Learner that all the words in the grid have a **long *ā*** sound.

- These are represented by the different letter combinations shown at the top of the page.

2. Ask your Learner to read each word in the grid.

- Tick all the words they get right. Leave the others blank.

3. When your Learner has finished, go over any words that have not been ticked.

- Read each of these words and sound them out and read again.
- Ask your Learner to read them again and tick the ones they get right.

4. Make a note of any words that are still a problem in the Notes box.

- Go over these words again once or twice.
- If any words remain a problem, or take two or three tries to get right, add them to the Parking page (page 157).

Tip:

Notes:

Read and check

Check that you can read these words with the **long a** sound

ay ai a _ e ei ey ea a

	✓
shade	
train	
away	
prey	
weight	
break	
Thursday	
danger	
plane	
paper	

	✓
stay	
fake	
eighty	
maintain	
taken	
survey	
maybe	
explain	
great	
freight	

	✓
Spain	
convey	
eight	
steak	
rebate	
lady	
reign	
they	
shame	
vein	

Words from page 73	✓

Text and check

Learners read sentences that include words with the **long ā** sound

1. Remind your Learner about all the letter combinations that make the **long ā** sound shown at the top of the Learner page.

2. Ask your Learner to read the sentences in the grid.
- Tick all the ones they get right and leave the others blank.

3. Go over sentences that have not been ticked.
- Underline any errors in each sentence.
- Read them to your Learner.
- Ask your Learner to read the sentences again and tick the ones they get right.

4. Make a note of any words that are still a problem in the Notes box. Go over these words once or twice.
- If any words remain a problem, or take two or three tries to get right, add them to the Parking page (page 157).

5. Ask your Learner to tell you what the text is about in their own words. Ask them questions to check understanding such as: What was wrong with Shane's luggage? Why was it so heavy?

Tip: Point out the pronunciation of the word **foreign**. The spelling follows the **long ā** pattern but is pronounced ***un*** in this case.

Notes:

Text and check

Read some sentences that have words with the **long a** sound

ay ai a _ e ei ey ea a	✓
I had arranged to meet my mate Shane at the airport station.	
He was coming in by train. We were going to Spain on our first foreign holiday to have a great time away from the rain.	
He came in on time and we made our way to the check-in desk.	
Everything was fine until he put his case on the conveyor. The lady was amazed at the weight of it.	
'That's way overweight!' she exclaimed. 'You'll have to pay extra I'm afraid.'	
'We'll repack it straight away,' I said. We didn't want to pay for excess baggage.	
I lifted the case off the conveyor but I had to strain to lift it up.	
'What have you got in the case, mate?' I asked. 'It feels like lead weights.'	
'That's right,' said Shane, 'I'm in training and it seems a shame to stop just because we're going away so I put my weights in.'	

Listen and point

Learners listen and find words with the **long ē** sound

1. Tell your Learner they are going to learn more about the **long ē** sound. Remind them of the letter combinations they have already learned: **ee** (tr**ee**), **ea** (m**ea**n), **y** (happ**y**), **e _ e** (**eve**).

- Ask your Learner to read the 4 lists at the top of the Learner page: **ee**, **ea**, **y** and **e _ e**.

2. Point out that there are more letter combinations that also make a **long ē** sound: **ey, ie, ei, e,** and **i** (all pronounced with **long ē**).

- Point to the letter combination **ey** and say the sound: **ē**. Read the **ey** list of words emphasising the **long ē** sound.
- Point to each word as you read it and ask your Learner to repeat the word.
- Go through the same list at random, say the words and ask your Learner to find and point to the correct word each time.

3. Go through the other lists in the same way.

4. Read words from any of the lists at random. Ask your Learner to find and point to the correct word in each case.

Tip: Some letter combinations make more than one sound such as **ey** (**long ā** in th**ey**; **long ē** in mon**ey**. Encourage your Learner to try both ways to see which works. Also point out the **short u** sound in m**o**ney.

Notes:

Listen and point

Learn more about the **long e** sound

ee	**ea**	**y**	**e _ e**
tr**ee**	m**ea**n	happ**y**	**e**v**e**
st**ee**r	pl**ea**	ver**y**	P**e**t**e**
b**ee**n	**ea**r	marr**y**	extr**e**m**e**
str**ee**t	w**ea**k	famil**y**	athl**e**t**e**
fift**ee**n	b**ea**ch	part**y**	th**e**m**e**

All the letters in bold say **long e**

ey	**ie**	**ei**	**e**	**i**
k**ey**	rel**ie**f	rec**ei**ve	m**e**	ser**i**ous
chimn**ey**	bel**ie**ve	dec**ei**ve	sh**e**	happ**i**ness
mon**ey**	calor**ie**	c**ei**ling	r**e**form	fur**i**ous
jock**ey**	p**ie**ce	conc**ei**ve	w**e**	empt**i**ness
kidn**ey**			d**e**lay	

Read and check

Learners practise reading words with the **long ē** sound

1. Point out to your Learner that all the words in the grid have a **long ē** sound.

- These are represented by the different letter combinations shown at the top of the page.

2. Ask your Learner to read each word in the grid.

- Tick all the words they get right. Leave the others blank.

3. When your Learner has finished, go over any words that have not been ticked.

- Read each of these words and sound them out and read again.
- Ask your Learner to read them again and tick the ones they get right.

4. Make a note of any words that are still a problem in the Notes box.

- Go over these words again once or twice.
- If any words remain a problem, or take two or three tries to get right, add them to the blank column on page 87. Your Learner can practise them when you reach that page.

Tip:

Notes:

Read and check

Check that you can read these words with the **long e** sound

ee ea y e _ e ey ie ei e i

	✓
tr**ee**	
m**ea**t	
ver**y**	
extr**e**m**e**	
k**ey**	
rel**ie**f	
rec**ei**ve	
happ**i**ness	
sh**e**	
eight**ee**n	

	✓
fear	
family	
athlete	
kidney	
calorie	
deceive	
emptiness	
delete	
street	
weak	

	✓
marry	
eve	
jockey	
piece	
ceiling	
serious	
reform	
seem	
chimney	
party	

Spot the sound

Learners look for the letter combinations that make the **long ē** sound

The first part of the text has been marked as an example.

1. Remind your Learner of all the letter combinations that can make the **long ē** sound.

- Tell them that they will be looking for these letter combinations in the text.

2. Read through the first 2 paragraphs and point out the letter combinations that make **long ē**. These have been marked in bold.

3. Ask your Learner to read the rest of the text with you.

- Ask them to look over the text again and underline any of the **long ē** sounds they can find.
- Show your Learner how to track along each line using their finger to find the **long ē** sounds.

4. Tell your Learner there is a **long ē** sound in the word **people** which they have learned as a Sight Word – it is an unusual spelling of **long ē**.

- Ask your Learner to find the word **people** in the text and underline it.

Tip: This is the longest piece of text that your Learner has been asked to read. Share the reading or read with your Learner.

Notes:

Spot the sound

Find the **long e** sound

ee	**ea**	**y**	**e _ e**	**ey**	**ie**	**ei**	**e**	**i**

Bleak Heath

It was a cl**ea**r day when w**e** set off across Bl**ea**k H**ea**th, but the mist came down and w**e** lost our path. **E**ve and I stumbled on. Our f**ee**t sank d**ee**p into the p**ea**t and w**e** b**e**gan to f**ee**l ver**y** w**ea**k. It got dark and b**e**gan to rain. W**e** f**ea**red that w**e** couldn't k**ee**p going much longer. This was getting s**e**r**i**ous.

Just then a light app**ea**red n**ea**rby. W**e** crept towards it and found a small, cr**ee**p**y** shack with smoke curling up from the chimn**ey**. W**e** p**ee**red in the window: an old woman sat hunched in a chair chuckling in a w**ei**rd way.

Suddenly there was a terrible scream and we turned to run but the door opened before we could get away. The old woman called to us. 'Don't leave,' she said. 'I don't see many people up here on the heath.'

We could see now that she was just a sweet old lady.

'Poor dears,' she said. 'You must be lost. Have a cup of tea and join me. I'm watching a scary horror film on TV. I love it.'

What a relief to be safe but it just goes to show how first impressions can deceive you.

Read and check

Learners practise reading words with the **long ē** sound

1. Point out to your Learner that all the words in the grid have a **long ē** sound.
- These are represented by the different letter combinations shown at the top of the page.

2. Ask your Learner to read each word in the grid.
- Tick all the words they get right. Leave the others blank.

3. When your Learner has finished, go over any words that have not been ticked.
- Read each of these words and sound them out and read again.
- Ask your Learner to read them again and tick the ones they get right.

4. Make a note of any words that are still a problem in the Notes box.
- Go over these words again once or twice.

5. If any words remain a problem, or take two or three tries to get right, add them to the Parking page (page 157).

Tip:

Notes:

Read and check

Check that you can read these words with the **long e** sound

ee   ea   y   e _ e   ey   ie   ei   e   i

	✓
we	
key	
relief	
happiness	
receive	
mean	
street	
party	
extreme	
very	

	✓
plea	
eve	
sixteen	
kidney	
bee	
curious	
ear	
believe	
serious	
chimney	

	✓
deceive	
jolly	
delete	
athlete	
cockney	
tweet	
perceive	
reach	
reform	
complete	

Words from page 83	✓

Text and check

Learners read sentences that include words with the **long ē** sound

1. Remind your Learner about all the letter combinations that make the **long ē** sound.

2. Ask your Learner to read the sentences in the grid.
- Tick all the ones they get right and leave the others blank.

3. Go over any sentences that have not been ticked.
- Underline any errors in each sentence.
- Read them to your Learner.
- Ask your Learner to read the sentences again and tick the ones they get right.

4. Make a note of any words that are a problem in the Notes box. Go over these words once or twice.
- If any words remain a problem, or take two or three tries to get right, add them to the Parking page (page 157).

5. Ask your Learner to tell you what the text is about in their own words. Ask some questions to check understanding such as: How many people came for a meal? Who was best at Cheat?

Tip:

Notes:

Text and check

Read some sentences that have words with the **long e** sound

ee ea y e _ e ey ie ei e i	✓
My partner Steve and I decided to have the family round for a meal on Christmas Eve.	
There were fifteen of us which was a bit of a squeeze.	
I haven't seen my niece Rita for ages and we were really pleased to meet her husband Rakesh and their new baby Deeta. She's a real sweetie.	
Steve and I looked at lots of recipes but in the end we settled for a big meat pie with mash, peas and gravy. It was really good.	
My Auntie Sally brought some wine and Uncle Terry brought some beer. The kids had fizzy drinks.	
We had cheesecake for sweet and after that we had tea and coffee. It was a real feast.	
After the meal we played the card game Cheat. My mum was the best. She deceived us all!	
We cleared up and went to bed very pleased with ourselves. It was a relief that it all went so well.	
'The key to a good evening is good grub and good people!' Steve said happily.	

Listen and point

Learners listen and find words with the **long ī** sound

1. Tell your Learner they are going to learn more about the **long ī** sound. Remind them of the letter combinations they have already learned: **y** (fl**y**), **igh** (n**igh**t remind them the **gh** is silent), **i - e** (k**i**t**e**).

- Ask your Learner to read the 3 lists at the top of the Learner page: **y**, **igh** and **i _ e**.

2. Point out that there are more letter combinations that also make a **long ī** sound: **ie, i** and **ei**.

- Point to the letter combination **ie** and say the sound: **ī**. Read the **ie** list of words emphasising the **long ī** sound.
- Point to each word as you read it and ask your Learner to repeat the word.
- Go through the same list at random, say the words and ask your Learner to find and point to the correct word each time.

3. Go through the other lists in the same way. Point out that the letter combination **ei** saying **long ī** is unusual and that **neither** and **either** are sometimes pronounced with a **long ē** as well.

4. Read words from any of the lists at random. Ask your Learner to find and point to the correct word in each case.

Tip: Where the same letter combination makes different sounds such as **ie** (**long ē** in p**ie**ce; **long ī** in p**ie**), encourage your Learner to try both ways to see which makes sense.

Notes:

Listen and point

Learn more about the **long i** sound

y	**igh**	**i _ e**
fl**y**	n**igh**t	k**i**t**e**
cr**y**	fl**igh**t	wh**i**t**e**
den**y**	r**igh**t	t**i**l**e**
appl**y**	h**igh**	wh**i**l**e**
suppl**y**	s**igh**	w**i**f**e**

All the letters in bold say **long i**

ie	**i**	**ei**
p**ie**	v**i**rus	h**ei**ght
t**ie**	**i**dea	n**ei**ther
cr**ie**s	s**i**lent	**ei**ther
fr**ie**d	m**i**cron	
repl**ie**d	f**i**nd	

Read and check

Learners practise reading words with the **long ī** sound

1. Point out to your Learner that all the words in the grid have a **long ī** sound.
- These are represented by the different letter combinations shown at the top of the page.

2. Ask your Learner to read each word in the grid.
- Tick all the words they get right. Leave the others blank.

3. When your Learner has finished, go over any words that have not been ticked.
- Read each of these words and sound them out and read again.
- Ask your Learner to read them again and tick the ones they get right.

4. Make a note of any words that are still a problem in the Notes box.
- Go over these words again once or twice.

5. If any words remain a problem, or take two or three tries to get right, add them to the blank column on page 97.

Tip:

Notes:

Read and check

Check that you can read these words with the **long i** sound

y igh i _ e ie i ei

	✓
fl**y**	
n**igh**t	
k**i**t**e**	
p**ie**	
v**i**rus	
h**ei**ght	
either	
s**i**lent	
fr**ie**d	
wh**i**t**e**	

	✓
apply	
flight	
wife	
light	
cries	
idea	
neither	
micron	
replied	
while	

	✓
sight	
supply	
why	
high	
fine	
pilot	
denied	
comply	
die	
final	

Spot the sound

Learners look for the letter combinations that make the **long ī** sound

The first part of the text has been marked as an example.

1. Remind your Learner of all the different letter combinations that can make the **long *ī*** sound.

- Tell them that they will be looking for these letter combinations in the text on the Learner page.

2. Read through the first 2 paragraphs and point out the letter combinations that make the **long *ī*** sound. These have been marked in bold.

3. Ask your Learner to read the rest of the text with you.

4. Ask them to look over the text again and underline any of the **long *ī*** sounds they can find.

- Show your Learner how to track along each line using their finger to find the **long *ī*** sounds.

Tip: Ask your Learner if they think the details in the text are fact (true) or fiction (made up)? (Fact: these names, dates, places are not made up.)

Notes:

Spot the sound

Find the **long i** sound

y   igh   i _ e   ie   i   ei

First Flight

For many years men tr**ie**d to fl**y** with balloons, k**i**t**e**s and gl**i**ders. They did go qu**i**t**e** h**igh** but there was never much control over the aircraft. There were many crashes and men d**ie**d tr**y**ing to fl**y**.

In December 1903 Orville Wr**igh**t flew the Fl**y**er for 12 seconds in North Carol**i**na USA. He flew at a h**ei**ght of 120 feet. This was the first manned aircraft to fl**y** under its own power. It was the first t**i**me that a p**i**lot was able to steer and balance the aircraft.

The Wright brothers were great inventors and pioneers. They based their ideas on bicycles because they believed that a pilot needed to steer and balance an aircraft like a bicycle while it was in flight. They tried many different designs before they got it right.

Now people fly at great speeds and heights all over the world.

Read and check

Learners practise reading words with the **long ī** sound

1. Point out to your Learner that all the words in the grid have a **long *ī*** sound.

- These are represented by the different letter combinations shown at the top of the page.

2. Ask your Learner to read each word in the grid.

- Tick all the words they get right. Leave the others blank.

3. When your Learner has finished, go over any words that have not been ticked.

- Read each of these words and sound them out and read again.
- Ask your Learner to read them again and tick the ones they get right.

4. Make a note of any words that are still a problem in the Notes box.

- Go over these words again once or twice.
- If any words remain a problem, or take two or three tries to get right, add them to the Parking page (page 157).

Tip:

Notes:

Read and check

Check that you can read these words with the **long i** sound

y igh i _ e ie i ei

	✓
flight	
mine	
fries	
frighten	
virus	
reply	
height	
bike	
try	
pie	

	✓
silent	
fly	
quite	
delight	
idea	
high	
denies	
cycle	
sight	
polite	

	✓
swipe	
deny	
fright	
white	
dies	
either	
light	
wife	
minus	
cries	

Words from page 93	✓

Text and check

Learners read sentences that include words with the **long ī** sound

1. Remind your Learner about all the letter combinations that make the **long ī** sound.

2. Ask your Learner to read the sentences in the grid.

- Tick all the ones they get right and leave the others blank.

3. Go over sentences that have not been ticked.

- Underline any errors in each sentence.
- Read them to your Learner.
- Ask your Learner to read the sentences again and tick the ones they get right.

4. Make a note of any words that are a problem in the Notes box. Go over these words once or twice.

- If any words remain a problem, or take two or three tries to get right, add them to the Parking page (page 157).

5. Ask your Learner to tell you what the text is about in their own words. Ask them questions to check understanding such as: When did the storm hit Twyford? What had happened to Mr Arkright's shed?

Tip:

Notes:

Text and check

Read some sentences that have words with the **long i** sound

Lightning strikes lucky for Mr Arkright	✓
At midnight last Friday Mr Arkright was woken by the violent storm that swept across Twyford.	
Mr Arkright was terrified by the wild weather as it crashed around his house.	
He was frightened that his house would not survive the battering of the high winds and rain.	
A sudden, massive bolt of lightning struck close to the house.	
Mr Arkright described it as a great fireball of bright light which hit his shed outside.	
'I was blinded by the light,' said Mr Arkright. 'It really hurt my eyes.'	
Finally the storm subsided and Mr Arkright was able to see the damage.	
His shed was now a pile of rubble but Mr Arkright was cheerful in spite of his ordeal.	
'I've been meaning to get rid of that shed for a while,' he said brightly. 'It was a lucky strike for me really.'	

Listen and point

Learners listen and find words with the **long ō** sound

1. Tell your Learner they are going to learn more about the **long ō** sound. Remind them of the letter combinations they have already learned: **oa** (b**oa**t), **ow** (gr**ow**), **o _ e** (h**o**m**e**).

- Ask your Learner to read the 3 lists at the top of the Learner page: **oa**, **ow**, **o _ e**.

2. Point out to your Learner that there are other letter combinations that also make a **long ō** sound: **oe, o, ough** and **ew** (all pronounced with **long ō**). These are less common.

- Point to the letter combination **oe** and say the sound: **ō**
- Read the **oe** list of words emphasising the **long ō** sound.
- Point to each word as you read it and ask your Learner to repeat the word.
- Go through the same list at random, say the words and ask your Learner to find and point to the correct word in each case.

3. Now go through the other lists in the same way.

4. Read words from any of the lists at random and ask your Learner to find and point to the correct word in each case.

Tip: Point out that the **long ō** represented by **ew** is rare – just one word here: sew. **ough** is also an unusual spelling of **long ō**.

Notes:

Listen and point

Learn more about the **long o** sound

oa	**ow**	**o _ e**
b**oa**t	gr**ow**	h**o**m**e**
gr**oa**n	wind**ow**	fr**o**z**e**
c**oa**ch	bel**ow**	v**o**t**e**
r**oa**d	wid**ow**	th**o**s**e**
c**oa**st	**ow**n	dr**o**v**e**

All the letters in bold say **long o**

oe	**o**	**ough**	**ew**
t**oe**	**o**pen	th**ough**	s**ew**
f**oe**	g**o**	alth**ough**	
J**oe**	b**o**ny	d**ough**	
tipt**oe**	ch**o**sen	d**ough**nut	

Read and check

Learners practise reading words with the **long ō** sound

1. Point out to your Learner that all the words in the grid have a **long ō** sound.
- These are represented by the different letter combinations shown at the top of the page.

2. Ask your Learner to read each word in the grid.
- Tick all the words they get right. Leave the others blank.

3. When your Learner has finished, go over any words that have not been ticked.
- Read each of these words and sound them out and read again.
- Ask your Learner to read them again and tick the ones they get right.

4. Make a note of any words that are still a problem in the Notes box.
- Go over these words again once or twice.

5. If any words remain a problem, or take two or three tries to get right, add them to the blank column on page 107. Your Learner can practise them again when you reach that page.

Tip:

Notes:

Read and check

Check that you can read these words with the **long o** sound

oa   ow   o _ e   oe   o   ough   ew

	✓
b**oa**t	
h**ome**	
gr**ow**	
t**oe**	
th**ough**	
s**ew**	
thr**ow**	
par**ole**	
open	
J**oe**	

	✓
froze	
doughnut	
road	
tiptoe	
those	
woe	
although	
boast	
zero	
suppose	

	✓
foe	
spoke	
hello	
foam	
pony	
choke	
dough	
go	
approach	
sew	

Spot the sound

Learners look for the letter combinations that make the **long ō** sound

The first part of the text has been marked as an example.

1. Remind your Learner of all the different letter combinations that can make the **long ō** sound.

- Tell them that they will be looking for these letter combinations in the text on the Learner page.

2. Read through the first paragraph and point out the letter combinations that make **long ō**. These have been marked in bold.

3. Ask your Learner to read the rest of the text with you.

4. Ask them to look over the text again and underline any of the **long ō** sounds they can find in the unmarked section.

- Show your Learner how to track along each line using their finger to find the **long ō** sounds.

Tip: Ask your Learner who is telling this story. (The nephew.)

Notes:

Spot the sound

Find the **long o** sound

oa **ow** **o _ e** **oe** **o** **ough** **ew**

I dr**o**v**e** to my uncle's **o**ld house on the c**oa**st. It stood on its **ow**n, high up on the cliffs away from the r**oa**d. My Uncle J**oe** left the house to me – his **o**nly nephew. He lived on his **ow**n and died al**o**n**e** in the house th**ough** n**o**-one really kn**ow**s how he died. It was years ag**o**. I supp**o**s**e** he just died of **o**ld age.

As I approached the house it looked very creepy but I don't believe in ghosts! The place was a mess but I was hopeful that I could renovate it and make it my home.

That night the wind was blowing and the old house creaked and groaned. The windows rattled and far below I could hear the waves crashing on the stony beach.

I liked the sound though and felt at home as I dozed off.

'Tomorrow I'll clean the place and mend the broken windows,' I spoke to myself. 'I will soon have a home of my own, thanks to Uncle Joe.'

Read and check

Learners practise reading words with the **long ō** sound

1. Point out to your Learner that all the words in the grid have a **long ō** sound.

- These are represented by the different letter combinations shown at the top of the page.

2. Ask your Learner to read each word in the grid.

- Tick all the words they get right. Leave the others blank.

3. When your Learner has finished, go over any words that have not been ticked.

- Read each of these words and sound them out and read again.
- Ask your Learner to read them again and tick the ones they get right.

4. Make a note of any words that are still a problem in the Notes box.

- Go over these words again once or twice.
- If any words remain a problem, or take two or three tries to get right, add them to the Parking page (page 157).

Tip:

Notes:

Read and check

Check that you can read these words with the **long o** sound

oa	**ow**	**o _ e**	**oe**	**o**	**ough**	**ew**

	✓
spoke	
dough	
slow	
foe	
code	
float	
snow	
suppose	
total	
approach	

	✓
below	
boat	
no	
home	
tiptoe	
although	
bonus	
shown	
bone	
ghost	

	✓
road	
toe	
though	
moment	
smoke	
throat	
throw	
sew	
doughnut	
so	

Words from page 103	✓

Text and check

Learners read sentences that include words with the **long ō** sound

1. Remind your Learner about all the letter combinations that make the **long ō** sound.

2. Ask your Learner to read the sentences in the grid.
- Tick all the ones they get right and leave the others blank.

3. Go over sentences that have not been ticked.
- Underline any errors in each sentence.
- Read them to your Learner.
- Ask your Learner to read the sentences again and tick the ones they get right.

4. Make a note of any words that are still a problem in the Notes box. Go over these words once or twice.
- If any words remain a problem, or take two or three tries to get right, add them to the Parking page (page 157).

5. Ask your Learner to tell you what the text is about in their own words. Ask them questions to check understanding such as: Why do you think Tony's voice came out as whisper the second time? (It went dry because he was scared.)

Tip: Remind your Learner that **dg** in **trudged** makes a **soft *g*** sound.

Notes:

Text and check

Read some sentences that have words with the **long o** sound

oa ow o _ e oe o ough	✓
It was a cold, frozen, snowy night. Tony trudged his way home in the full moon. His hands and toes were freezing.	
As Tony approached his house, he heard a rustling noise in the trees by his gate.	
He spoke in a loud voice, 'Hello, who's there?' Tony tiptoed closer. He spoke again.	
'Who's there?' His throat was so dry it came out as a whisper this time.	
Although Tony was scared he began to open the gate. It squeaked on its rusty hinges.	
A streak of red fur rushed past Tony and fled along the road.	
'Well that's a relief, it's just my old foe the fox,' said Tony as he opened his front door.	
'Now for a hot drink and a sit in front of an open fire to warm me up.'	

Listen and point

Learners listen and find words with the **long ū** sound

1. Tell your Learner they are going to learn more about the **long *ū*** sound. Remind them of the letter combinations they have already learned: **ue** (tr**ue**), **oo** (sh**oo**t, t**oo**k), **ew** (f**ew**), **u _ e** (c**u**b**e**).

- Ask your Learner to read the 4 lists at the top of the Learner page: **ue**, **oo**, **ew**, **u _ e**.

2. Point out to your Learner that there are other letter combinations that also make a **long *ū*** sound: **ou**, **o**, **u** and **ui**.

- Point to the letter combination **ou** and say the sound: ***ū*** (as in y**ou**).
- Read the **ou** list of words emphasising the **long *ū*** sound.
- Point to each word as you read it and ask your Learner to repeat the word.
- Go through the same list at random, say the words and ask your Learner to find and point to the correct word in each case.

3. Now go through the other lists in the same way.

4. Read words from any of the lists at random and ask your Learner to find and point to the correct word in each case.

Tip: Point out that the **long *ū*** represented by **o** is rare but **do**, **to**, **who** and **two** are commonly used words.

Notes:

Listen and point

Learn more about the **long u** sound

ue	**oo**	**ew**	**u _ e**
tr**ue**	sh**oo**t	f**ew**	c**u**b**e**
bl**ue**	b**oo**k	d**ew**	t**u**b**e**
stat**ue**	sm**oo**th	kn**ew**	cr**u**d**e**
val**ue**	t**oo**th	ch**ew**	p**u**r**e**
tiss**ue**	ch**oo**se	gr**ew**	f**u**s**e**

All the letters in bold say **long u**

ou	**o**	**u**	**ui**
s**ou**p	d**o**	s**u**per	j**ui**ce
gr**ou**p	t**o**	m**u**sic	s**ui**t
c**ou**pon	wh**o**	r**u**by	fr**u**it
w**ou**nd	tw**o**	n**u**merous	br**ui**se
sh**ou**ld		L**u**cy	

Read and check

Learners practise reading words with the **long ū** sound

1. Point out to your Learner that all the words in the grid have a **long ū** sound.
- These are represented by the different letter combinations shown at the top of the page.

2. Ask your Learner to read each word in the grid.
- Tick all the words they get right. Leave the others blank.

3. When your Learner has finished, go over any words that have not been ticked.
- Read each of these words and sound them out and read them again.
- Ask your Learner to read them again and tick the ones they get right.

4. Make a note of any words that are still a problem in the Notes box.
- Go over these words again once or twice.
- If any words remain a problem, or take two or three tries to get right, add them to the blank column on page 117. Your Learner can practise them again when you reach that page.

Tip: Remind your Learner that they have learnt **could** and **would** as Sight Words.

Notes:

Read and check

Check that you can read these words with the **long u** sound

ue   oo   ew   u _ e   ou   o   u   ui

	✓
tr**ue**	
t**o**	
gr**ew**	
m**u**sic	
sh**oo**t	
r**u**d**e**	
kn**ew**	
t**u**b**e**	
w**oo**d	
fr**ui**t	
sh**ou**ld	

	✓
suit	
ruby	
wound	
few	
issue	
stood	
troop	
crude	
look	
new	
would	

	✓
do	
soon	
cube	
soup	
school	
gloom	
super	
group	
juice	
two	
could	

Spot the sound

Learners look for the letter combinations that make the **long ū** sound

The first part of the text has been marked as an example.

1. Remind your Learner of all the different letter combinations that can make the **long ū** sound.

- Tell them that they will be looking for these letter combinations in the text on the Learner page.

2. Read through the first paragraph and point out the letter combinations that make **long ū**. These have been marked in bold.

3. Ask your Learner to read the rest of the text with you.

4. Ask them to look over the text again and underline any of the **long ū** sounds they can find in the unmarked section.

- Show your Learner how to track along each line using their finger to find the **long ū** sounds.

Tip: Remind your Learner that the **long ū** sound can be longer as in **troop** and **flew** or shorter as in **stood** and **would**.

Notes:

Spot the sound

Find the **long u** sound

ue	**oo**	**ew**	**u _ e**	**ou**	**o**	**u**	**ui**

The tr**oo**p of soldiers in **u**niform st**oo**d with their heads bowed. An air of gl**oo**m came over the crowd of onl**oo**kers as they st**oo**d watching the procession. Children in sch**oo**l **u**niform held hands. They kn**ew** that things w**ou**ld never be the same in their village again. The army band played a t**u**n**e** that s**ui**ted the occasion.

The funeral of ten men took place today. Twelve days ago no one knew that a disaster was about to take place that would take the lives of so many men.

That day started at the army base and was part of a usual training routine for new recruits. The recruits knew that the routine involved taking them out in a Sea King helicopter over the Irish Sea and taking part in an evacuation exercise in Ireland. It would then be a flight back to base.

Some say it was the sea fog and poor visibility that caused the crash; others assume it was engine failure. The investigation by the army will pursue many avenues in order to come up with the truth.

Read and check

Learners practise reading words with the **long ū** sound

1. Point out to your Learner that all the words in the grid have a **long *ū*** sound.

- These are represented by the different letter combinations shown at the top of the page.

2. Ask your Learner to read each word in the grid.

- Tick all the words they get right. Leave the others blank.

3. When your Learner has finished, go over any words that have not been ticked.

- Read each of these words and sound them out and read again.
- Ask your Learner to read them again and tick the ones they get right.

4. Make a note of any words that are still a problem in the Notes box.

- Go over these words again once or twice.
- If any words remain a problem, or take two or three tries to get right, add them to the Parking page (page 157).

Tip: Some accents put a ***y*** sound on **united**.

Notes:

Read and check

Check that you can read these words with the **long u** sound

ue   oo   ew   u _ e   ou   o   u   ui

	✓
true	
few	
tune	
today	
broom	
unit	
should	
cruise	
rescue	
bruise	

	✓
united	
stood	
would	
blue	
knew	
wood	
do	
uniform	
exclude	
could	

	✓
who	
issue	
flew	
tube	
juice	
soon	
statue	
suit	
choose	
truth	

Words from page 113	✓

Text and check

Learners read sentences that include words with the **long ū** sound

1. Remind your Learner about all the letter combinations that make the **long *ū*** sound.

2. Ask your Learner to read the sentences in the grid.
- Tick all the ones they get right and leave the others blank.

3. Go over sentences that have not been ticked.
- Underline any errors in each sentence.
- Read them to your Learner.
- Ask your Learner to read the sentences again and tick the ones they get right.

4. Make a note of any words that are a problem in the Notes box. Go over these words once or twice.
- If any words remain a problem, or take two or three tries to get right, add them to the Parking page (page 157).

5. Ask your Learner to tell you what the text is about in their own words. Ask questions to check understanding such as: Why did the fans stand in silence? (An old player had died.) What does a red card do? (It sends them off for the match).

Tip: Point out **one thing's** in Sentence 7 and remind your Learner that it is the shortened form of **one thing is**. Remind them of other short forms such as: what's, there's, I'll, she'll, isn't.

Notes:

Text and check

Read some sentences that have words with the **long u** sound

ue **oo** **ew** **u _ e** **ou** **o** **u** **ui**	✓
The Manchester United fans stood up at the start of the match.	
They all knew that this was a suitable way of saying goodbye to an old player who had just died at the age of seventy-two.	
Manchester City fans with their blue scarves also stood as a mark of respect.	
The tune from the band ended the silence. The players flew into their positions.	
The whistle blew and a huge roar went up as the match began.	
To tell the truth, both teams were great but it was too soon to know who would win.	
One thing's for certain, no-one wanted to get a red card and be excluded from this crucial match.	
It was a blur of red and blue and a goal was scored!	

Spot the word

Learners look for the Sight Words: **laugh**, **enough**, **won't**, **wash**, **water**, **pretty**

This task relies on whole word recognition.

1. Read the words: **laugh, enough, won't, wash, water, pretty.**
- Ask your Learner to read the words.

2. Show your Learner how to search the small boxes for the word: **laugh.**
- Tick the word every time you find it (there are 3). Write the number on the notepad.

3. Ask your Learner to search the small boxes for the word: **enough.**
- Tick the word every time they find it (there are 3). Write the number on the notepad.

4. Do the same for the other words: **won't** (3), **wash** (2), **water** (2), **pretty** (3).

Tip: There are 3 words beginning with **w** in this activity. Show your Learner how to use word shape or other parts of the word to help find each word such as: the apostrophe in **won't**.

Notes:

Spot the word

Read and match the Sight Words

laugh	enough	won't	wash	water	pretty

water pretty laugh

won't won't

laugh enough

wash wash

enough

pretty pretty

water

won't laugh

enough

laugh ______________

enough ______________

won't ______________

wash ______________

water ______________

pretty ______________

Read and check

Learners practise reading Sight Words

1. Remind your Learner that Sight Words need to be remembered as whole words not sounded out.

2. Ask your Learner to read each word in the grid.

- Tell them to tick all the words they get right and leave the others blank.

3. When your Learner has finished, go over any words that have not been ticked:

- Read them to your Learner (do not sound them out).
- Ask your Learner to read them again and tick the ones they get right.

4. If any words remain a problem, or take two or three tries to get right, write them in the Notes box and practise them with 'Look and Say, Copy and Say' (as you do on the Parking page) until your Learner is confident.

Tip:

Notes:

Read and check

Check that you can read these Sight Words

	✓
laugh	
enough	
won't	
wash	
water	
pretty	
wash	
enough	
won't	
pretty	
water	

	✓
laugh	
wash	
enough	
water	
won't	
wash	
laugh	
pretty	
water	
enough	
won't	

Text and check

Learners read sentences with Sight Words

1. Ask your Learner to read the Sight Words: **laugh, enough, won't, wash, water, pretty.**

- Practise the words with your Learner if you need to.

2. Ask your Learner to read the sentences in the grid.

- Tick all the ones they get right and leave the others blank.

3. Go over any sentences that have not been ticked.

- Underline any errors in each sentence.
- Read them to your Learner.
- Ask your Learner to read the sentences again and to tick the ones they get right.

4. Make a note of any words that are a problem in the Notes box. Go over these once or twice.

- If any words remain a problem, or take two or three tries to get right, add them to the Parking page (page 157).

5. Ask questions about the sentences to check understanding such as: What did Jenny need hot water for? Who went for a coffee?

Tip:

Notes:

Text and check

Read some sentences with Sight Words

laugh	enough	won't	wash	water	pretty

	✓
My friend and I went for a coffee and had a good laugh together.	
'There's not enough hot water for me to wash up,' Jenny said.	
The pretty girl made him laugh all the time.	
'I won't sing if you are going to laugh at me!' said his daughter.	
My son loves to swim in water but he won't wash if he can help it.	
My auntie had enough cloth left to make me a pretty skirt.	
The dress was very pretty but the label said you have to wash it by hand.	
It will be a long walk so make sure you have enough water.	
My father won't be stuck at home now that he has a new car.	
There won't be enough time to make the cake pretty but it will taste just as good.	

Listen and point

Learner listen and find words with the **or** sound

1. Tell your Learner they are going to learn more about the ***or*** sound. Remind them of the letter combinations they have already learned: **or** (f**or**), **ore** (m**ore**), **aw** (y**aw**n), **au** (fr**au**d).
- Ask your Learner to read the 4 lists at the top of the Learner page: **or**, **ore**, **aw**, **au**.

2. Point out that there are other letter combinations that also make an ***or*** sound: **oar, oor, ough, ar, our** (all pronounced with an ***or*** sound, as in f***or***). These are less common.
- Point to the letter combination **oar** and say the sound: ***or***
- Read the **oar** list of words emphasising the ***or*** sound.
- Point to each word as you read it and ask your Learner to repeat the word.
- Go through the same list at random, say the words and ask your Learner to find and point to the correct word in each case.

3. Now go through the other lists in the same way.

4. Read words from any of the lists at random and ask your Learner to find and point to the correct word in each case.

Tip: Point out the ***or*** sound represented by **ar,** comes mostly after a **w**: **war, warm, wart, swarm**. Note that some of these sounds may be different in some accents.

Notes:

Listen and point

Learn more about the **or** sound

or	**ore**	**aw**	**au**
f**or**	m**ore**	j**aw**	l**au**nch
gl**or**y	sc**ore**	dr**aw**	fr**au**d
s**or**t	sh**ore**	s**aw**n	h**au**nt
sp**or**t	bef**ore**	fl**aw**	l**au**ndry
sh**or**t	st**ore**	y**aw**n	**Au**gust

All the letters in bold say **or**

oar	**oor**	**ough**	**ar**	**our**
b**oar**d	fl**oor**	f**ough**t	w**ar**m	c**our**t
oar	d**oor**	th**ough**t	w**ar**	c**our**se
h**oar**d	m**oor**	br**ough**t	w**ar**t	y**our**
r**oar**	p**oor**	s**ough**t	sw**ar**m	
s**oar**			rew**ar**d	

Read and check

Learners practise reading words with the **or** sound

1. Point out to your Learner that all the words in the grid have an ***or*** sound.

- These are represented by the different letter combinations shown at the top of the page.

2. Ask your Learner to read each word in the grid.

- Tick all the words they get right. Leave the others blank.

3. When your Learner has finished, go over any words that have not been ticked.

- Read each of these words and sound them out and read again.
- Ask your Learner to read them again and tick the ones they get right.

4. Make a note of any words that are still a problem in the Notes box.

- Go over these words again once or twice.
- If any words remain a problem, or take two or three tries to get right, add them to the blank column on page 133. Your Learner can practise them again when you reach that page.

Tip:

Notes:

Read and check

Check that you can read these words with the **or** sound

or	**ore**	**aw**	**au**	**oar**	**oor**	**ough**	**ar**	**our**

	✓
r**oar**	
m**oor**	
th**ough**t	
w**ar**m	
f**or**m	
s**oar**ing	
t**ore**	
t**au**nting	
sw**ar**m	
l**au**ndry	

	✓
launch	
flooring	
store	
board	
wart	
brought	
court	
haunt	
sought	
toward	

	✓
sawn	
fought	
course	
ward	
hoard	
lawn	
fraud	
poor	
August	
more	

Spot the sound

Learners look for the letter combinations that make the **or** sound

The first part of the text has been marked as an example.

1. Remind your Learner of all the different letter combinations that can make the ***or*** sound.

- Tell them that they will be looking for these letter combinations in the text on the Learner page.

2. Read through the first paragraph and point out the letter combinations that make the ***or*** sound. These have been marked in bold.

3. Ask your Learner to read the rest of the text with you.

4. Ask them to look over the text again and underline any of the ***or*** sounds they can find in the unmarked text.

- Show your Learner how to track along each line using their finger to find the ***or*** sounds.

Tip: Ask your Learner if they think the text is fact (real/true) or fiction (made up)? (Fact: it is about a real person and gives true details.)

Notes:

Spot the sound

Find the **or** sound

or	**ore**	**aw**	**au**	**oar**	**oor**	**ough**	**ar**	**our**

David Attenborough is one of our greatest naturalists. He ign**ore**s all w**ar**nings about expl**or**ing difficult and dangerous parts of the world. In his expl**or**ations he has s**ough**t out h**oar**ds of rare animals, plants, trees and creatures. He has often s**ough**t out h**au**nts that would make y**our** j**aw** drop in horr**or** if you were there!

In his many television series, David Attenborough has brought raw nature into our living rooms as he transports us around the globe. Of course, before these shows we had to rely on books for most of our information. We now have a hoard of information for years to come caught on film.

Whether it's on a seashore, a Scottish moor or the deepest jungle, David and his film crew's patience brings its reward. We are able to watch nature in all its glory, without stepping further than our own front door.

Read and check

Learners practise reading words with the **or** sound

1. Point out to your Learner that all the words in the grid have an ***or*** sound.

- These are represented by the different letter combinations shown at the top of the page.

2. Ask your Learner to read each word in the grid.

- Tick all the words they get right. Leave the others blank.

3. When your Learner has finished, go over any words that have not been ticked.

- Read each of these words and sound them out and read again.
- Ask your Learner to read them again and tick the ones they get right.

4. Make a note of any words that are still a problem in the Notes box.

- Go over these words again once or twice.
- If any words remain a problem, or take two or three tries to get right, add them to the Parking page (page 157).

Tip:

Notes:

Read and check

Check that you can read these words with the **or** sound

or	**ore**	**aw**	**au**	**oar**	**oor**	**ough**	**ar**	**our**

	✓
sorted	
flaw	
more	
board	
score	
August	
adore	
shore	
brought	
warning	

	✓
warm	
forget	
pause	
jaw	
door	
court	
soared	
glory	
toward	
autumn	

	✓
stormy	
thawing	
roaring	
moor	
before	
thought	
drawing	
floor	
course	
reward	

Words from page 129	✓

Text and check

Learners read sentences that include words with the **or** sound

1. Remind your Learner about all the letter combinations that make the ***or*** sound.

2. Ask your Learner to read the sentences in the grid.
- Tick all the ones they get right and leave the others blank.

3. Go over sentences that have not been ticked.
- Underline any errors in each sentence.
- Read them to your Learner.
- Ask your Learner to read the sentences again and tick the ones they get right.

4. Make a note of any words that are a problem in the Notes box. Go over these words once or twice.
- If any words remain a problem, or take two or three tries to get right, add them to the Parking page (page 157).

5. Ask your Learner to tell you what the text is about in their own words. Ask them questions to check understanding such as: Where is the festival held? Which day of the week do the public have a go on the track?

Tip:

Notes:

Text and check

Read some sentences that have words with the **or** sound

or **ore** **aw** **au** **oar** **oor** **ough** **ar** **our**	✓
Rory couldn't wait for the end of May to come when the Isle of Man TT races begin.	
It was his best sport even though he had broken his leg and jaw last year.	
He brought his family to the motorbike festival every year and this year was no different, except that he was not a competitor any more.	
He remained, however, a very staunch supporter of the sport.	
Rory loved to hear the roar of the engines as they came screeching towards him and the warm applause from the crowd.	
These sounds brought back memories of the time he broke the lap record and went home in glory.	
This would be a most enjoyable fortnight even if the weather had some storms in store for them.	
The public get their chance to roar around the track on what is called 'Mad Sunday'.	
People are allowed to do laps of the course and, as Rory knows, they do not crawl along!	

Listen and point

Learners listen and find words with the **er** sound

1. Tell your Learner they are going to learn more about the ***er*** sound. Remind them of the letter combinations they have already learned: **er** (lett**er**), **ur** (b**ur**n), **ir** (b**ir**d).

- Ask your Learner to read the 3 lists at the top of the Learner page: **er**, **ur** and **ir**.

2. Point out that there are more letter combinations that also make an ***er*** sound: **our**, **or**, **ear** and **ar**.

- Point to the letter combination **our** and say the sound: ***er***. Read the **our** list of words emphasising the ***er*** sound.
- Point to each word as you read it and ask your Learner to repeat the word.
- Go through the same list at random, say the words and ask your Learner to find and point to the correct word each time.

3. Go through the other lists in the same way. Point out that **our**, **or** and **ar** are often at the end of two or three-syllable words.

4. Read words from any of the lists at random. Ask your Learner to find and point to the correct word in each case.

Tip: Point out that in words that end with **sure** the **s** is pronounced with a ***zh*** sound: mea***s***ure lei***s***ure, expo***s***ure, clo***s***ure.

Notes:

Listen and point

Learn more about the **er** sound

er	ur	ir
h**er**	h**ur**t	b**ir**d
lett**er**	expos**ure**	d**ir**ty
f**er**n	n**ur**se	st**ir**
mak**er**	s**ur**prise	th**ir**d
sist**er**	meas**ure**	c**ir**cus
	b**ur**st	

All the letters in bold say **er**

our	or	ear	ar
col**our**	w**or**d	**ear**th	coll**ar**
flav**our**	doct**or**	**ear**ly	cust**ar**d
od**our**	visit**or**	h**ear**d	cell**ar**
lab**our**	act**or**	s**ear**ch	regul**ar**
hum**our**	w**or**k	l**ear**n	popul**ar**

Read and check

Learners practise reading words with the **er** sound

1. Point out to your Learner that all the words in the grid have an ***er*** sound.
- These are represented by the different letter combinations shown at the top of the page.

2. Ask your Learner to read each word in the grid.
- Tick all the words they get right. Leave the others blank.

3. When your Learner has finished, go over any words that have not been ticked.
- Read each of these words and sound them out and read again.
- Ask your Learner to read them again and tick the ones they get right.

4. Make a note of any words that are still a problem in the Notes box.
- Go over these words again once or twice.
- If any words remain a problem, or take two or three tries to get right, add them to the blank column on page 143. Your Learner can practise them when you reach that page.

Tip:

Notes:

Read and check

Check that you can read these words with the **er** sound

er **ur** **ir** **our** **or** **ear** **ar**

	✓
h**er**b	
earn	
b**ur**nt	
col**our**	
w**or**d	
s**ur**prise	
earth	
b**ir**d	
butt**er**	
pill**ar**	
meas**ure**	

	✓
learn	
search	
matter	
flavour	
turn	
doctor	
standard	
walker	
birthday	
vapour	
closure	

	✓
exposure	
shirt	
stern	
beggar	
labour	
her	
dollar	
early	
purpose	
work	
popular	

Spot the sound

Learners look for the letter combinations that make the **er** sound

The first part of the text has been marked as an example.

1. Remind your Learner of all the different letter combinations that can make an ***er*** sound.

- Tell them that they will be looking for these letter combinations in the text on the Learner page.

2. Read through the first 2 paragraphs and point out the letter combinations that make an ***er*** sound. These have been marked in bold.

3. Ask your Learner to read the rest of the text with you.

4. Ask them to look over the text again and underline any of the ***er*** sounds they can find.

- Show your Learner how to track along each line using their finger to find the ***er*** sounds.

Tip: Ask your Learner some questions about the text to check understanding such as: What did the inspector have for pudding? How many years had the cafe been open?

Notes:

Spot the sound

Find the **er** sound

er **ur** **ir** **our** **or** **ear** **ar**

A rum**our** had been h**ear**d in the cafe that a food inspect**or** was going to call any day.

The own**er**s, F**er**n and Matt, w**er**e very conc**er**ned that their little cafe, in its th**ir**d year of op**er**ation, might not come up to the food and hygiene stand**ar**ds expected. Their regul**ar** custom**er**s told them not to worry. The cafe was a great place with food full of flav**our**.

The next day F**er**n nudged Matt as a tall, st**er**n-looking man ent**er**ed the cafe and took a corn**er** seat. 'It's him, I'm c**er**tain,' said F**er**n. The man ordered a h**er**b-crusted lamb chop, roast potatoes and cabbage, followed by an apple pie with cust**ar**d.

When Fern went over to ask if everything was to his satisfaction, the man said, 'An excellent meal full of flavour! But first I have to tell you I'm a food inspector so I do need to look in your kitchen and carry out a detailed search.'

'Of course, come this way,' said Fern.

Half an hour later, the inspector returned and shook hands with Fern and Matt, 'You fully deserve your Food Hygiene Certificate. You can expect lots of regular customers if you go on serving food of such a high standard.' Fern and Matt gave out free drinks to everyone to honour the occasion.

Read and check

Learners practise reading words with the **er** sound

1. Point out to your Learner that all the words in the grid have the ***er*** sound.

- These are represented by the different letter combinations shown at the top of the page.

2. Ask your Learner to read each word in the grid.

- Tick all the words they get right. Leave the others blank.

3. When your Learner has finished, go over any words that have not been ticked.

- Read each of these words and sound them out and read again.
- Ask your Learner to read them again and tick the ones they get right.

4. Make a note of any words that are still a problem in the Notes box.

- Go over these words once or twice.
- If any words remain a problem, or take two or three tries to get right, add them to the Parking page (page 157).

Tip:

Notes:

Read and check

Check that you can read these words with the **er** sound

er   ur   ir   our   or   ear   ar

	✓
turn	
worm	
stern	
cellar	
flavour	
early	
operator	
burglar	
behaviour	
birthday	

	✓
purpose	
earth	
measure	
herb	
research	
yearned	
thirteen	
deserve	
perhaps	
burden	

	✓
humour	
sister	
heard	
learned	
work	
pleasure	
certain	
bird	
search	
furniture	

Words from page 139	✓

Text and check

Learners read sentences that include words with the **er** sound

1. Remind your Learner about all the letter combinations that make an ***er*** sound.

2. Ask your Learner to read the sentences in the grid.
- Tick all the ones they get right and leave the others blank.

3. Go over sentences that have not been ticked.
- Underline any errors in each sentence.
- Read them to your Learner.
- Ask your Learner to read the sentences again and tick the ones they get right.

4. Make a note of any words that are a problem in the Notes box. Go over these words once or twice.
- If any words remain a problem, or take two or three tries to get right, add them to the Parking page (page 157).

5. Ask your Learner to tell you what the text is about in their own words. Ask them questions to check understanding such as: What was it that came to town? What was it Victor had told them?

Tip: Ask your Learner to find and point to any sentences where there is someone speaking. (There are 3. This is shown by the speech marks ‘ ’ .)

Notes:

Text and check

Read some sentences that have words with the **er** sound

er **ur** **ir** **our** **or** **ear** **ar**	✓
The circus arrived early one wet morning and set up on the outskirts of Burton–on-Trent.	
The children first spotted the Big Top on their way home from school.	
They took it in turns to test their nerve to look inside and report back to the others what they had seen.	
Oliver said he had seen a wizard, Mansur had heard a lion roaring and Victor said he had seen dogs jumping through some burning hoops.	
'You can't have heard a lion roar because this circus doesn't have wild animals,' said Taylor.	
That night the children came early and sat in the front row. They were nervous with excitement.	
'I hear the clowns throw custard pies at you if you sit in the front row,' whispered Mansur to the others.	
It wasn't custard they got covered with, it was water. The clowns squirted them from coloured hose pipes.	
Next, hoops were set on fire and dogs with ruffled collars hurled themselves through the flames.	
'See, what did I tell you!' said Victor with a smug grin.	

Listen and point

Learners listen and find words with the **ul** sound

1. Tell your Learner they are going to learn more about the ***ul*** sound. Remind them of the letter combinations they have already learned: **le** (hand**le**), f**ul** (usef**ul**), **al** (med**al**).

- Ask your Learner to read the 3 lists at the top of the Learner page: **le**, **ful** and **al**.

2. Point out that there are more letter combinations which also make an ***ul*** sound at the end of a word: **ol**, **el**, and **il** (all pronounced ***ul*** as in f***ull***).

- Point to the letter combination **ol** and say the sound: ***ul***. Read the **ol** list of words emphasising the ***ul*** sound.
- Point to each word as you read it and ask your Learner to repeat the word.
- Go through the same list at random, say the words and ask your Learner to find and point to the correct word each time.

3. Go through the other lists in the same way.

4. Read words from any of the lists at random. Ask your Learner to find and point to the correct word in each case.

Tip: Point out that when **ful** is at the end of a longer word it has one **l** and when it is a word on its own it has two: **full**.

Notes:

Listen and point

Learn more about the **ul** sound

le	ful	al
hand**le**	harm**ful**	med**al**
tab**le**	aw**ful**	met**al**
unc**le**	pain**ful**	loy**al**
sing**le**	law**ful**	capit**al**
app**le**	skil**ful**	sign**al**

All the letters in bold say **ul**

ol	el	il
id**ol**	funn**el**	ev**il**
petr**ol**	cru**el**	penc**il**
Brist**ol**	parc**el**	foss**il**
symb**ol**	pan**el**	lent**il**
pist**ol**	mod**el**	counc**il**

Read and check

Learners practise reading words with the **ul** sound

1. Point out to your Learner that all the words in the grid have an ***ul*** sound.
- These are represented by the different letter combinations shown at the top of the page.

2. Ask your Learner to read each word in the grid.
- Tick all the words they get right. Leave the others blank.

3. When your Learner has finished, go over any words that have not been ticked.
- Read each of these words and sound them out and read again.
- Ask your Learner to read them again and tick the ones they get right.

4. Make a note of any words that are still a problem in the Notes box.
- Go over these words again once or twice.
- If any words remain a problem, or take two or three tries to get right, add them to the blank column on page 153. Your Learner can practise them when you reach that page.

Tip: Tell your Learner that the **le** ending is the most common spelling of this sound.

Notes:

Read and check

Check that you can read these words with the **ul** sound

le	**ul**	**al**	**ol**	**el**	**il**

	✓
midd**le**	
awf**ul**	
med**al**	
petr**ol**	
pan**el**	
penc**il**	
tab**le**	
lev**el**	
lent**il**	
id**ol**	

	✓
basil	
signal	
uncle	
pistol	
coastal	
hurtful	
rebel	
council	
terrible	
chapel	

	✓
kestrel	
useful	
nostril	
impossible	
model	
exceptional	
single	
symbol	
skilful	
fossil	

Spot the sound

Learners look for the letter combinations that make the **ul** sound

The first part of the text has been marked as an example.

1. Remind your Learner of all the different letter combinations that can make an ***ul*** sound.

- Tell them that they will be looking for these letter combinations in the text on the Learner page.

2. Read through the first 3 paragraphs and point out the letter combinations that make an ***ul*** sound. These have been marked in bold.

3. Ask your Learner to read the rest of the text with you. Remind them about syllable division if needed.

4. Ask them to look over the text again and underline any of the ***ul*** sounds they can find.

- Show your Learner how to track along each line using their finger to find the ***ul*** sounds.

Tip: Ask your Learner if this piece of text is fact or fiction. (Fact: names, places, times and other details are clues that this is a factual piece of text.)

Notes:

Spot the sound

Find the **ul** sound

le **ul** **al** **ol** **el** **il**

Brist**ol** is a bustling city in the south-west of England. It is famous for many things. Among these is the production of the remarkab**le** Concorde which was the first and only supersonic passenger plane.

Many pilots who flew on Concorde are still f**ull** of respect for this incredib**le** plane. Captain David Rowland of the Roy**al** Aeronautic**al** Society said that, 'Concorde was a delight to fly – a mod**el** aeroplane.'

He went on to say, 'I could get emotion**al** about it, even though it is not fashionab**le** in some politic**al** circ**le**s to celebrate it.'

His statement may puzzle some people. Why would this not be something to celebrate? After all, this wonderful plane could fly to the USA in less than three hours!

However, at these incredible speeds, Concorde used up vast amounts of aviation fuel and did possible damage to the atmosphere. The environmental cost was felt to be too great.

The first Concorde flew out of Bristol on 9th April 1969 on an inaugural flight of 22 minutes. The last Concorde flew into Bristol on 27th November 2003. Its final resting place.

Read and check

Learners practise reading words with the **ul** sound

1. Point out to your Learner that all the words in the grid have an ***ul*** sound.

- These are represented by the different letter combinations shown at the top of the page.

2. Ask your Learner to read each word in the grid.

- Tick all the words they get right. Leave the others blank.

3. When your Learner has finished, go over any words that have not been ticked.

- Read each of these words and sound them out and read again.
- Ask your Learner to read them again and tick the ones they get right.

4. Make a note of any words that are still a problem in the Notes box.

- Go over these words again once or twice.
- If any words remain a problem, or take two or three tries to get right, add them to the Parking page (page 157).

Tip:

Notes:

Read and check

Check that you can read these words with the **ul** sound

le ul al ol el il

	✓
settle	
petrol	
powerful	
panel	
medal	
pencil	
model	
cancel	
basil	
stumble	

	✓
coastal	
nostril	
simple	
council	
awful	
symbol	
circle	
chapel	
Bristol	
evil	

	✓
middle	
lentil	
idol	
signal	
kestrel	
skilful	
uncle	
impossible	
terrible	
fossil	

Words from page 149	✓

Text and check

Learners read sentences that include words with the **ul** sound

1. Remind your Learner about all the letter combinations that make an ***ul*** sound.

2. Ask your Learner to read the sentences in the grid.

- Tick all the ones they get right and leave the others blank.

3. Go over sentences that have not been ticked.

- Underline any errors in each sentence.
- Read them to your Learner.
- Ask your Learner to read the sentences again and tick the ones they get right.

4. Make a note of any words that are a problem in the Notes box. Go over these words once or twice.

- If any words remain a problem, or take two or three tries to get right, add them to the Parking page (page 157).

5. Ask your Learner some questions about the text to check understanding such as: What food is the kestrel mostly like to catch? Why do they fly south in the winter? (To get away from the cold and find more food.)

Tip:

Notes:

Text and check

Read some sentences that have words with the **ul** sound

le **ul** **al** **ol** **el** **il**	✓
It is a wonderful spectacle to watch a kestrel rise up on the air currents, then level off and hover high above the land in search of food on the ground.	
Kestrels prefer open spaces such as fields, scrubland, heaths and marshland that border coastal areas to catch their voles, mice and shrews.	
They sometimes catch several in a day to satisfy their own hunger and any growing chicks back in the nest.	
Kestrels have been known to catch spiders and beetles, especially on warm islands in the southern hemisphere where they are sensible enough to fly to in the winter.	
The kestrel is sometimes seen, like other birds of prey, as a symbol of the power of nature. It is a force to be reckoned with but a force for graceful energy, not evil.	

Parking page

Use the page opposite to note down any sounds or words you have come across in the manual that your Learner needs to practise again. Do this activity when you have completed all the other activities.

1. Write the words in the first (Park) column as you come across them in the manual.

2. When you and your Learner get to this page:

- Take **one** word at a time.
- Read it to your Learner and sound it out (Note: Sight Words are **not** sounded out).
- Ask your Learner to read the whole word.
- Ask your Learner to copy the word and say it.
- Tick it if they get it right.
- Repeat the whole process with the same word: Copy and Say, Copy and Say until they are confident with it. Repeat on a new row if you need to.

3. Repeat the 'Look and Say, Copy and Say' process with all the other words in the Park column.

4. If your Learner continues to struggle with a word, make sure they know what the words means and try putting it into sentences for them.

Tip:

Notes:

Park. Look and Say	✓

Copy and Say	✓

Copy and Say	✓

Copy and Say	✓

Parking page

Use the page opposite to note down any more words your Learner needs to practise again. Treat in the same way as outlined on the previous Parking page.

Tip:

Notes:

Park. Look and Say	✓

Copy and Say	✓

Copy and Say	✓

Copy and Say	✓

Progress check

Explain to your Learner that this is a good point in the programme to see how things are going.

Ask your Learner to read each word in the Progress check.

- Tick everything they get right.
- Leave blank any words that your Learner cannot read.
- Use the Turning Pages Reading Levels to show your Learner how much they have achieved.
- Keep a note of any words or letter sounds they are not confident with. Your Learner can practise them at the beginning of the next session.

Turning Pages Reading Levels

All or most of the words with the **long *ā*, *ē*, *ī*, *ō*, *ū*** sounds read correctly. (No more than 8 errors.)	**TP Level 5.6**
All or most of the Sight Words read correctly. (No more than 1 error.)	**TP Level 5.7**

Tip:

Notes:

Progress check

Read and tick all the words you know:

	✓		✓		✓
game		receive		open	
seem		fly		believe	
boast		straight		today	
paper		fear		very	
night		cube		through	
true		fine		theme	
explain		home		unit	
throw		survey		shook	
few		although		break	
die		juice		spooky	
eight		kidney		happiness	
toe		virus		delay	

	✓
water	
pretty	
won't	
laugh	
enough	
wash	

TP Level 5.6 ☐

TP Level 5.7 ☐

Progress check

Ask your Learner to read each word in the Progress check.

- Tick everything they get right.
- Leave blank any words that your Learner cannot read.
- Use the Turning Pages Reading Levels to show your Learner how much they have achieved.
- Keep a note of any words or letter sounds they are not confident with. Your Learner can practise them at the beginning of the next session.

Turning Pages Reading Levels

All or most of the words with the **er** and **or** sounds read correctly. (No more than 5 errors.)	**TP Level 5.8**
All or most of the words with the **ul** sound read correctly (No more than 5 errors.)	**TP Level 5.9**

If your Learner makes more than 20 errors overall you will need to go over the relevant activities again and spend some more time practising with the Turning Pages reading books. When you have done this, try the Progress check again.

Tip:

Notes:

Progress check

Read and tick all the words you know:

	✓		✓
worm		colour	
helicopter		course	
sorted		early	
soared		August	
roar		shore	
cellar		supporter	
bird		herb	
warn		thought	
burnt		brought	
swarm		flavour	
moor		thirteen	
hoard		flaw	

TP Level 5.8 ☐

	✓
middle	
scribble	
quarrel	
model	
evil	
hurtful	
coastal	
kestrel	
lentil	
petrol	
stressful	
pedal	

TP Level 5.9 ☐

Progress check feedback

The Turning Pages Reading Levels show your Learner what they have achieved.

Congratulate them and explain what each level means.

Ask your Learner if there any words that they would like to go over again. Make a note of them below.

Go over them before moving on.

Your Learner has achieved the skills to read all the Turning Pages reading books and other emergent reader materials available from the library.

Tip:

Notes:

Congratulations!

You are reading longer pieces of text with a wide range of sounds and spelling patterns. You are reading with understanding.

You are now reading at **TP Level 5.9**

Next we are going to look at different types of text and ways to read with confidence.

Reading

Learners use the layout of a menu to find information

1. Tell your Learner to look at the text on the Learner page.

- Ask them to tell you what the text is and what it is for. (A menu for people to choose what they want to eat each day.)

2. Point out the layout of the menu. Explain how the following things help you to find information:

- The table format breaks down the information into smaller chunks.
- The headings help the reader to find their way around: days of the week, LUNCH, DINNER. (In bold and in capital letters to show that they are important.)
- The symbols for different dietary needs: ☺ - Healthy eating, ♓ - Halal, ⌘ - Vegetarian.
- Tell your Learner that they can use these layout clues to find information, such as finding all the vegetarian meals using the symbols.

3. Ask your Learner to find and read the following:

- All the vegetarian options available for lunch on Tuesday.
- How many Halal options there are for dinner on Monday.
- A dish with beef in it for dinner on Tuesday.

Tip: Show your Learner how to **scan** the table by moving your finger from one part of the menu to another to find particular information. Read it aloud **in detail** when you find it.

Notes:

Use a menu to find information

Menu

Week beginning **AUGUST 9th**

Tick your choices and put the completed menu in the post boxes in the dining room by:

18.00 Hours FRIDAY

NAME:	**NUMBER:**	☺ Healthy eating ♓ Halal ⌘ Vegetarian

	LUNCH		✓	**DINNER**		✓
Monday	Cheese melt	♓ ⌘		Battered cod	♓	
	Ham and pickle salad	☺		Spicy chicken	♓ ☺	
	Vegetable burger	♓ ⌘ ☺		Lentil and mushroom bake	♓ ⌘ ☺	
	Sausage roll and beans			Cheese and onion flan	♓ ⌘	

	LUNCH		✓	**DINNER**		✓
Tuesday	Cajun tuna and peppers	♓ ☺		Fish fillet in parsley sauce	♓ ☺	
	Ham and onion sandwiches			Stir fry vegetables	♓ ⌘ ☺	
	Vegetable soup and roll	♓ ⌘ ☺		Beef casserole	☺	
	Falafel and pitta bread	♓ ⌘ ☺		Cheese and onion pasty	♓ ⌘	

Reading
Learners use the menu to find and read information

1. Tell your Learner that they are now going to use part of the menu to find information and decide if the statements on the Learner page are **true** or **false**.

2. Read the first statement. Show your Learner how to look for the information in the menu and decide together if it is true or false. Tick the correct column.

3. Tell your Learner to read the next statement, find the information and decide whether it is true or false.

- Remind them to use the headings and the symbols to help them.

4. Ask your Learner to do the same with the other statements.
   (1. True, 2. False, 3. False, 4. True, 5. True, 6. False.)

5. Ask your Learner to look at the full menu and make their own choices for lunch and dinner on Monday and Tuesday and complete the form.

Tip: Remind your Learner that text will often be smaller or in different styles in everyday texts.

Notes:

Menu

Week beginning **AUGUST 9th**
Tick your choices and put the completed menu in the post boxes in the dining room by:
18.00 Hours FRIDAY

NAME:	**NUMBER:**	☺ Healthy eating ♓ Halal Ж Vegetarian

Monday

LUNCH		✓
Cheese melt	♓ Ж	
Ham and pickle salad	☺	
Vegetable burger	♓ Ж ☺	
Sausage roll and beans		

DINNER		✓
Battered cod	♓	
Spicy chicken	♓ ☺	
Lentil and mushroom bake	♓ Ж ☺	
Cheese and onion flan	♓ Ж	

		True	False
1.	Ham and pickle salad is a healthy eating option.		
2.	The menu must be completed and returned to the post box by Tuesday afternoon.		
3.	Sausage roll and beans is a healthy option.		
4.	Lentil and mushroom bake is suitable for all diets.		
5.	Spicy chicken can be ordered for dinner on Monday.		
6.	There is a fish dish on offer for lunch and dinner on Monday.		

Reading

Learners read instructions

1. Ask your Learner to look at the text on the Learner page.

- Ask them to read the text and tell you what it is. (Instructions for taking a medicine.)
- Ask them what helped them to know. (Name of the product, the layout – bullet points, information in boxes, words in bold.)
- Explain to your Learner how this type of **layout** helps you to find important information quickly and to read it accurately.

2. Ask if it's important to read these instructions in **detail**. (Yes, especially if the medicine has not been given to you by a doctor.)

3. Ask your Learner to read all the instructions again in detail.

4. Ask your Learner to answer these questions (they may need to scan the text again to find the answers):

- Can a 3-year-old child take this medicine? (No – 6 years and upwards.)
- How many tablets can an 8-year-old child take? (Half to one, 4 times a day.)
- Why would a person take these tablets? (For fast pain relief.)
- Is it all right for an elderly person to take this medicine? (Yes.)
- When should you take the medicine? (Mealtimes or with food.)

Tip: Ask your Learner to use the syllables to read the name of the medicine: Get/bett/a/mol

Notes:

Read these instructions

Getbettamol... *the path to fast pain relief*

How to take this medicine

Swallow the tablets with water at mealtimes or with food

Age	Dose and how often to take
Children from 6 to 12 years	Half to one tablet up to four times a day
Adults, the elderly and children over 12 years	Take 1 or 2 tablets up to four times a day

This medicine is NOT suitable for children under six years old

- Do not take this medicine more than 4 times in a day (24 hours).
- Do not take this medicine more often than every 4 hours.
- Do not take more tablets than the label tells you.
- Do not take for more than 3 days unless instructed by your doctor.

You **MUST** contact your doctor or health provider:

- If you do not get better in 3 days.
- If you take too much of this medicine. (This medicine can have a serious effect on your liver.)
- If you have any side-effects from taking this medicine.

Reading

Learners read instructions

1. Tell your Learner that they are going to read part of the instructions for taking a medicine and decide if the statements on the Learner page are **true** or **false**.

2. Point out the bullet points. Explain that these are often used to break down complex information into easier chunks to read and understand.

- Point out the key words: **do not** and **MUST**. Stress how important it is to read the instructions carefully whenever they see these words.

3. Remind them that they will need to **scan** for specific information and then read what they find **in detail** in order to answer true or false.

4. Ask your Learner to tick true or false to the questions in the grid. (Answers: 1. False, 2. True, 3. True, 4. False, 5. True, 6. True)

Tip: If your Learner is not sure of any answers, read the instructions through with them, pointing out the key bits that will help.

Notes:

This medicine is NOT suitable for children under six years old

- Do not take this medicine more than 4 times in a day (24 hours).
- Do not take this medicine more often than every 4 hours.
- Do not take more tablets than the label tells you.
- Do not take for more than 3 days unless instructed by your doctor.

You **MUST** contact your doctor or health provider:

- If you do not get better in 3 days.
- If you take too much of this medicine. (This medicine can have a serious effect on your liver.)
- If you have any side-effects from taking this medicine.

		True	False
1.	This medicine has no side-effects.		
2.	You can take it for longer if your doctor tells you to.		
3.	You must not take the medicine more than 4 times in a day.		
4.	You can take the medicine every 2 hours if you need to.		
5.	You should see a doctor if you are not better in 3 days.		
6.	It is all right to see a health provider if you cannot see your doctor.		

Reading

Learners use the format of a dictionary to find information

1. Tell your Learner to look at the text.

- Ask them to tell you what the text is and what it is for. (Part of a **dictionary** which gives you the spellings and meanings of words.)

2. Point out the layout of the dictionary. Explain how the following things help you to find information:

- The **table format** breaks down the information into smaller chunks.
- Words are **grouped together** using the first letters in the word. (These words all begin with **ph**.)
- The **words are in bold** to help you choose which one to look at in detail and to separate the word from its meaning (definition).

Tell your Learner that they can use these layout clues to find information.

3. Ask your Learner to find and read the following:

- What word is **phone** short for? (Telephone.)
- A **photograph** can be stored in two ways. Name one of these ways. (Paper or electronically.)
- What is a fear of spiders called? (Arachnophobia – a/ra**ch**/no/pho/bi/a – **ch** sounds like a ***k***.)
- Which word describes learning to read by matching sounds to letters? (Phonics.)

Tip: If possible, show your Learner a dictionary and support them to use it.

Notes:

Word (ph)	Definition
phobia	An extreme fear or dislike of something such as arachno**phobia** – the fear of spiders.
phone	Short for tele**phone**. A system for transmitting the human voice over a distance using wires or radio.
phonics	A method of learning to read by matching sounds to letters or letter combinations. Turning Pages is a phonic reading programme.
photograph	A picture made with a camera. The image can be stored on paper, using chemicals or electronically, using a digital process.

Reading

Learners use the layout of a dictionary to find information

1. Tell your Learner that they are going to find more information from a section of a dictionary.

- Ask them if a dictionary contains **fact** or **fiction** and why. (Fact: it gives the spellings and explains the meanings of words.)

2. Ask your Learner to answer **yes** or **no** to the following questions:

- Do you have to read every word in a dictionary? (No – it is a reference book to find specific information.)
- Does it help to know the order of letters in the alphabet? (Yes – you look up a word by using the order of the alphabet (a – z) such as finding the word: **m**entor by starting at the **m** section of the dictionary.)
- Can you scan the page to find what you want? (Yes – scanning is when you are looking for specific information or key words. You don't have to read the whole page in detail.)
- After scanning do you have to use detailed reading? (Yes – words that look similar are close together on the page.)

3. Ask your Learner to read the text in detail to answer the questions. (1. agoraphobia, 2. acrophobia, 3. insectophobia, 4. technophobia.)

Tip: Your Learner does not need to write out the answers to Question 5. Ask them to give the meanings in their own words.

Notes:

Reading

Use a dictionary to find information

Word (ph)	Definition	Example words
phobia	An extreme fear or dislike of something such as arachno**phobia** – the fear of spiders.	insecto**phobia** – fear of insects techno**phobia** – fear of technology agora**phobia** – fear of open spaces acro**phobia** – fear of heights
phone	Short for tele**phone**. A system for transmitting the human voice over a distance using wires or radio.	tele**phone** micro**phone** head**phones**

	Use the dictionary	Answer
1.	People with this phobia don't like open spaces.	
2.	People with this phobia would not choose to work on high buildings.	
3.	People with this phobia do not like insects.	
4.	Some people love it, some hate it and some fear it. What is it called when you have a fear of technology?	
5.	Tell your Mentor your own definition of the words microphone and headphones.	

Reading

Learners read a formal letter

1. Ask your Learner to look at the text on the Learner page.

- Ask them to read it and tell you what it is. (A formal letter.)
- Ask them what helped them to know it was a letter. (The address, Dear Mr Smith, Yours sincerely.)
- Remind your Learner that the **layout** helps us to know what to expect to read in the text.
- Point out that a **formal** letter (sent by an outside organisation like this one from the hospital) always follows a set layout.
- Point out the font style which is often used for formal letters.
- Ask if it is important to read a letter like this in **detail**. (Yes because it has important information about times and places for an appointment.)

2. Ask your Learner to read the letter in detail and find the answers to these questions:

- Which department is Mr Smith going to? (Ear, Nose and Throat.)
- What should Mr Smith do if he cannot make this appointment? (Phone or go online.)
- When is Mr Smith's appointment? (Thursday 2nd July 2015 at 10.15 am.)
- Which doctor is Mr Smith going to see? (Mr Hajek.)

Tip: Point out the formal style in the last sentence: ...may result in your being...

Notes:

Lowtown Hospital
Lowtown
FR1 0RF

Private and confidential
12 May 2025

NHS Patient Number: ZZZZZ33330

Dear Mr Smith

An appointment has been made for you to attend the outpatient clinic for a review of your condition on:

Thursday 2nd July 2025 at 10.15 am. with **Mr Hajek** in the **Ear, Nose and Throat Department**.

Please bring this letter with you and report to the reception desk in the **Main Outpatients Department**. Please bring with you a list of all your current medication.

If you are unable to attend at this time or if you would like to change your appointment, please telephone the appointments line on: 0500 050505 as soon as possible. You can also contact us through the CHOOSE AND BOOK service online www.chooseandbook.nhs.uk

Failure to attend this appointment without prior notification may result in your being removed from our waiting list.

Yours sincerely
Booking Clerk

Reading

Learners read a formal letter

1. Tell your Learner that they are going to look again at part of the letter about a hospital appointment.

2. Remind them that they will need to **scan** for specific information and then read what they find **in detail** in order to answer the multiple-choice questions at the bottom of the page.

3. Ask your Learner to tick: **a**, **b**, or **c** as the correct answer to the questions in the grid. (1. **a**, 2. **b**, 3. **c**, 4. **a**)

4. If your Learner is not sure of any answers then read the letter through with them, pointing out the key bits that will help.

- Use a finger to reveal the telephone number a chunk at a time if your Learner is finding it tricky to decide the answer to Question 3.

Tip: Remind your Learner that if they don't get the meaning of the text on first reading to read it again a couple of times.

Notes:

Please bring this letter with you and report to the reception desk in the **Main Outpatients Department**. Please bring with you a list of all your current medication.

If you are unable to attend at this time or if you would like to change your appointment, please telephone the appointments line on: 0500 050505 as soon as possible. You can also contact us through the CHOOSE AND BOOK service online www.chooseandbook.nhs.uk

Failure to attend this appointment without prior notification may result in your being removed from our waiting list.

Yours sincerely
Booking Clerk

1. Where do you go to first when you get to the hospital Main Outpatients Department?	a) The reception desk b) The booking clerk c) The Choose and Book service
2. What could happen if you cannot keep your appointment and you do not let them know?	a) You are given another one b) You could be removed from the waiting list c) You are never seen again
3. The appointments phone line is:	a) 0050 050550 b) 0500 500505 c) 0500 050505
4. What should you do about any medication you are taking?	a) Write a list of them and bring this information with you b) Phone and give them the information c) Bring all the medication with you

Reading

Learners read a recipe

1. Ask your Learner to look at the text on the Learner page.

- Ask them to read the text and tell you what it is. (A recipe.)
- Ask them how they know what it is. (Headings, list of ingredients, numbering of the instructions.)
- Point out that a **recipe** nearly always follows a set layout: ingredients first followed by the method of preparing and cooking.

2. Ask if it's important to read a recipe in **detail.** (Yes but any recipe can be changed depending on the confidence and taste of the cook.)

3. Ask your Learner to read the recipe again in detail and find the answers to these questions:

- What is the main ingredient of a risotto? (Rice.)
- How should the chicken stock be added? (A little at a time.)
- Is this risotto cooked in the oven? (No – it's cooked in a pan on the hob.)
- What does it mean when it says add salt and pepper to taste? (As much as the cook likes.)
- What is veg short for? Point out the ***soft g*** (saying ***j***). (Veg is short for vegetables.)

Tip: Talk about any favourite foods or recipes you both may have.

Notes:

Simple Risotto

Ingredients

1 medium onion
Olive oil or butter (2 tablespoons)
Risotto rice (2 cups)
1 glass dry white wine (optional)
Chicken stock (4 cups)
Parmesan cheese
Salt and pepper

Method

1. Finely slice one onion and fry it in light oil until soft. (Don't put the heat too high.)
2. Add 2 cups of risotto rice to the pan. Stir it in with the fried onions for a short while until the rice grains are all shiny with oil.
3. Turn the heat up slightly and add (optional) dry white wine.
4. Now add chicken stock a little at a time. Keep stirring until the stock has been absorbed. (You will need 4 cups of stock.)
5. Add salt and pepper to taste and slices of Parmesan cheese.
6. Scatter with chopped chives or basil to finish or spice it up with other nice veg such as peas or peppers.

Reading

Learners read a recipe in detail

1. Tell your Learner that they are going to look again at part of the risotto recipe.
- Tell them they are going to read the numbered instructions (the Method)

2. Explain to your Learner that the instructions for making and cooking the risotto are shown again at the bottom of the page, but they are in the wrong order.
- Tell them to put these instructions into the right order by numbering them correctly.
- Point out that one has already been done.
- Point out that this activity can be done by **scanning** for **key words** – finding and matching the first 2 words of every instruction.

3. Tell them to read the text again **in detail** to check they have done it correctly.

4. The answers are: **5. 3. 6. 1. 4. 2.**

5. If your Learner is not sure of any answers then read the recipe extract through with them, pointing out the key words that start each instruction.

Tip: Tick each instruction as it is found in the recipe, so it is easier to see which ones are still left to be numbered.

Notes:

Simple Risotto

Method

1. Finely slice one onion and fry it in light oil until soft. (Don't put the heat too high.)
2. Add 2 cups of risotto rice to the pan. Stir it in with the fried onions for a short while until the rice grains are all shiny with oil.
3. Turn the heat up slightly and add (optional) dry white wine.
4. Now add chicken stock a little at a time. Keep stirring until the stock has been absorbed. (You will need 4 cups of stock.)
5. Add salt and pepper to taste and slices of Parmesan cheese.
6. Scatter with chopped chives or basil to finish or spice it up with other nice veg such as peas or peppers.

	These instructions are out of order. Put them in order by numbering them.
5.	Add salt and pepper to taste and slices of Parmesan cheese.
	Turn the heat up slightly and add (optional) dry white wine.
	Scatter with chopped chives or basil to finish or spice it up with other nice veg such as peas or peppers.
	Finely slice one onion and fry it in light oil until soft. (Don't put the heat too high.)
	Now add chicken stock a little at a time. Keep stirring until the stock has been absorbed. (You will need 4 cups of stock.)
	Add 2 cups of risotto rice to the pan. Stir it in with the fried onions for a short while until the rice grains are all shiny with oil.

Reading

Learners read a job profile

1. Ask your Learner to look at the text on the Learner page.

- Ask them to **skim** read the text and tell you what it is. (A job profile.)
- Ask them what helped them to know it was a job description. (Title, the list of bullet points.)
- Tell your Learner that the **title** is the main clue to know what to expect to read in the text.
- Point out that a **job profile** generally follows a set layout but this can be different depending on the job.

2. Ask your Learner to read the job profile in detail and find the answers to these questions:

- Is this an actual job description or a general description of what it takes to become an instructor? (General description or Job Profile.)
- What words tell you that the job may vary from place to place? (You may ...)
- Name 2 of the qualities you need to be a good fitness instructor. (Keen on health and fitness; enjoy meeting people; be able to motivate and inspire.)

Tip: Ask your Learner what other information they would expect to find if this was a job profile about a specific job. (Place, hours, pay, responsibilities.)

Notes:

Job Profile Fitness Instructor

A fitness instructor leads people in exercise activities.
You must be keen on health and fitness, and enjoy meeting people.
You need to motivate and inspire people.

The work:

You may work in gyms, fitness clubs, leisure centres, hotels or holiday resorts.
You may work with groups or individuals.
Your job may include:

- doing fitness assessments and introduction sessions for new customers
- showing customers how to use equipment or weights
- giving advice about healthy eating and exercise
- leading group exercise sessions such as Zumba, kick boxing, swimming or spinning
- cleaning and maintaining equipment

Qualifications:

There are many opportunities in the fitness industry to get qualifications.
You can train on the job or study at college.

Reading

Learners read a job profile with multi-syllable words

1. Tell your Learner that they are going to look again at part of the job profile. They are going to read about **the work** itself.

2. Tell your Learner that some words have been highlighted in the text to show that they have 1, 2, 3, 4 or 5 syllables.
   - Show how these words have been recorded in the grid below.

3. Tell your Learner to look through the text again and find 3 more words with only 1 syllable. Ask them to underline them and write them in the table.

4. Now ask your Learner to look through the text again and find:
   - 3 more words with 2 syllables
   - 3 more words with 3 syllables

   Remind them to tap out the words in order to hear the number of 'beats' (syllables).

5. Ask your Learner to look again at the full profile on page 187 to see if they can find any other words with more than 3 syllables for example: activities (4), qualifications (5), opportunities (5).

Tip:

Notes:

Reading

Read a job profile with multi-syllable words

The work:

You may work in gyms, fitness clubs, leisure centres, hotels or holiday resorts.
You may work with groups or individuals.
Your job may include:

- doing fitness assessments and introduction sessions for new customers
- showing customers how to use equipment or weights
- giving advice about healthy eating and exercise
- leading group exercise sessions such as Zumba, kick boxing, swimming or spinning
- cleaning and maintaining equipment

1 syllable	2 syllables	3 syllables	4 syllables	5 syllables
you	fit/ness	hol/i/day	in/tro/duc/tion	in/di/vi/du/als

Reading

Learners read a factual piece of text and scan for information

1. Tell your Learner to look at the text on the Learner page.
- Point out the different font style particularly the **g**.
- Ask them to **look at the layout of the text** (no detailed reading at this stage) and tell you what they notice. (Title, bullet points, some words in bold.)
- Ask them if they have picked up any of the information from the page just from this quick look at the text such as: what the title says. If not, reassure them that it is fine as they are now going to read it.

2. Ask your Learner to read the text.
- You can support them by sharing the reading (take it in turns to read) or reading together, with your voice quietly providing background support.
- Ask your Learner what the text is about. (How dogs were used in the war.)

3. Ask your Learner to **scan** the text for **specific information** such as:
- Which dogs were strong enough to pull supplies in a cart?
- Which dogs were used to kill the rats in the trenches?

Tip: Remind your Learner that they have **scanned** for text in earlier manuals and can **scan** for key words: **supplies** and **rats**.

Notes:

Reading

Read the text using scanning skills

The Dogs of War

Dogs were used by all sides in the First World War for many different jobs:

- **Sentry dogs** were used to patrol military camps. They worked with one guard and were trained to growl or bark when there were strangers about. Dobermans were perfect for this job and are still used as guard dogs today.
- **Scout dogs** worked with soldiers on foot. They could detect the enemy scent at 1,000 yards. They did not bark but would stiffen and indicate the direction of the enemy. They helped many patrols enter enemy territory undetected.
- **Mercy dogs** were trained to find injured and dying soldiers on the battlefield. They carried medical supplies so that men could help themselves. They stayed with soldiers in their dying moments.
- **Messenger dogs** could run faster than men and could cope with the rough terrain in the trenches. They were trained to carry important messages to and from headquarters. These dogs often got through when human runners would have failed.
- **Ratters** were all terriers. They were used to kill the rats that infested the trenches.
- **Supply dogs** were strong dogs that could pull a cart over rough terrain carrying ammunition and other supplies. Dogs were also used to lay down telegraph wires.

About a million dogs died in the battlefields of the First World War.

Reading

Learners read a factual piece of text to find information

1. Tell your Learner that they are now going to use part of the text about 'The Dogs of War' to find some information.

2. Tell them that they will need to **scan** the text for key words and to **read in detail** to find the answers.

3. Do Question 1 together. Read the question and tell your Learner that you are going to **scan** for the key word **foot** as a clue to the answer.

- Run your finger along the lines of text asking your Learner to look out for the word **foot**.
- Underline it when it is found in the **Scout dogs** section.
- Ask your Learner to read the sentence with the word **foot** in it and to write the answer **Scout dogs** in the space in the grid.

4. Ask your Learner to find the answers to the other questions. (1. Scout dogs, 2. Scout dogs, 3. Doberman, 4. Medical supplies, 5. First World War.)

- Remind them that if they cannot spot key words then they must read each dog description in detail.

Tip: Point out to your Learner that the text will often be smaller or in different styles in everyday texts.

Notes:

Reading

Read the text to find the answers

The Dogs of War

Dogs were used by all sides in the First World War for many different jobs:

- **Sentry dogs** were used to patrol military camps. They worked with one guard and were trained to growl or bark when there were strangers about. Dobermans were perfect for this job and are still used as guard dogs today.
- **Scout dogs** worked with soldiers on foot. They could detect the enemy scent at 1,000 yards. They did not bark but would stiffen and indicate the direction of the enemy. They helped many patrols enter enemy territory undetected.
- **Mercy dogs** were trained to find injured and dying soldiers on the battlefield. They carried medical supplies so that men could help themselves. They stayed with soldiers in their dying moments.

	Do you know?	**Answer**
1.	Which dogs worked with foot soldiers?	
2.	Which dogs did not bark when the enemy was near?	
3.	Which breed of dog still makes the best guard dog?	
4.	What did Mercy dogs take to injured soldiers?	
5.	In which war were dogs so useful?	

Progress check

Congratulate your Learner. They have now completed Turning Pages. It is a good time to have a final check of the reading skills they have learned.

1. Tell your Learner to have a brief look at the text on the Learner page and discuss the following questions:

- What type of text is this? How do they know? (Newspaper page, layout and headings.)
- What sort of information do they expect to find in this text? Stories, facts, information or entertainment? (All of these.)
- Would they normally read the whole thing word for word? (Unlikely.)
- How would they choose what to read? (Skim to find things of interest to them.)
- Is everything in a newspaper true? (No.)

2. Ask your Learner to look more closely at the page and answer these questions:

- How many news items are there on the page? (3)
- How many adverts are there on the page? (1)
- What is on this page that will help them to find other things in the newspaper? (Contents pages.)

The final progress check for your Learner is on pages 196 and 197. Ask your Learner to use the newspaper text to complete the questions on page 196. There are 14 questions and the answers are given on page 198. If your Learner gets 11 or more questions right they have achieved Turning Pages Level 6.0. If your Learner gets fewer than 11 questions right, discuss the errors and go over the relevant activities again until they feel confident enough to try the Progress check again.

Didbury Daily News

Friday January 9th 2015 | www.didburynews.com | Price 50p

Brave by name and brave by nature …

When Tom Devlin fell in the canal on his way to school last Tuesday he thought he would drown. He cannot swim and the filthy water of the Dorret Canal soon filled his lungs but luckily for him a hero was just around the corner. Arshan Nadeem arrived just in the nick of time to save Tom:

'I didn't have time to think,' said Arshan, 'I was on my way to work when I saw this lad struggling in the water. I jumped in straight away. I knew I had to help.'

Arshan was praised by the fire service for his prompt action. Fire Officer Ted Mills said that jumping into the cold, filthy water was a very brave act.

Arshan's mother told us: 'The name Arshan means brave and that's just what he is!'

Platinum bride!

Local couple Hetty Ford (92) and her devoted husband Albert, who is a spritely 95, celebrate seventy years of married bliss this week with a platinum anniversary party. Mr Ford said that when he married Hetty she was a platinum blonde but now she is true platinum grey just like the real thing.

Anti-Fracking Protest

News of plans to start fracking for shale gas in Didbury Heath has shocked local residents who are planning a protest march to the Town Hall next Thursday.

More on page 2 …

Also in this paper …

Progress check

Use this newspaper extract to answer these questions. Tick all the ones you get right.

Didbury Daily News	What date was this newspaper published?	
	How much does the paper cost?	
	Where will they find the quiz page?	
	Where will they find the sport?	
Brave by name, brave by nature	Who fell in the canal?	
	What was the name of the Fire Officer?	
	What does the name Arshan mean?	
	Did Arshan think twice before jumping into the water?	
Platinum bride	How old is Mr Ford?	
	Devoted means: a) Taking part in an election b) Very attached to someone c) Unwell	
	What colour is Hetty's hair now? a) Platinum blonde b) Platinum white c) Platinum grey	
Anti-fracking	Anti-fracking means that you are NOT in favour of fracking. **True/False**	
	The local residents want the fracking to start in Didbury Heath. **True/False**	
	There is more about this story in the paper. **True/False**	